The
Courage
to Dare

The
Courage
to Dare

The Spirituality of Catherine Donnelly,
Founder of the Sisters of Service

Kathryn Perry

Introduction by Mary Jo Leddy

NOVALIS

© 2013 Novalis Publishing Inc.

Cover design and layout: Audrey Wells
Interior images: pp. 5, 48, 122, 170: courtesy Sisters of Service Archives;
p. 32: Plaisted

Published by Novalis

Publishing Office
10 Lower Spadina Avenue, Suite 400
Toronto, Ontario, Canada
M5V 2Z2

Head Office
4475 Frontenac Street
Montréal, Québec, Canada
H2H 2S2
www.novalis.ca

Library and Archives Canada Cataloguing in Publication

Perry, Kathryn, 1958-   The courage to dare : the spirituality of Catherine
Donnelly, founder of the Sisters of Service / Kathryn Perry.

ISBN 978-2-89646-539-2

    1. Donnelly, Catherine, 1884-1983. 2. Sisters of Service--History.
3. Nuns--Canada--Biography. I. Title.

BX4237.P47 2013   271'.97   C2012-906716-4

Printed in Canada.

We acknowledge the financial support of the Government of Canada through the
Canada Book Fund for business development activities.

5   4   3   2   1   17   16   15   14   13

This book is dedicated to

Sister Catherine Donnelly, SOS,
Canadian missionary pioneer
and founder of the Sisters of Service of Canada

Catherine Donnelly in the 1950s

"I had to have the courage to dare ..."

Sister Catherine Donnelly,
Founder of the Sisters of Service

Acknowledgements

I am forever indebted to Catherine Donnelly, founder of the Sisters of Service of Canada. Her community of religious women has become a touchstone for me, helping me to connect with her spirit of generosity, faith, courage and commitment. While acknowledging my gratitude to all Sisters of Service for their willingness to share memories and details of their history with me, I owe particular thanks to Sisters Marilyn MacDonald, Adua Zampese, Anna McNally and Patricia Burke, who have been my primary contacts during the research and writing of this manuscript.

I express gratitude to Sisters of Service who generously shared their memories and insights about Catherine: Sisters Agnes Sheehan, Margaret Ready, Viola Mossey, Lena Renaud, Mary-Ellen Francoeur, Mary Halder, Frances Coffee, Helen Hayes, Hilda Lunney, Colleen Young, Bernice Anstett, Patsy Flynn, and Marilyn Gillespie. Sister Anita Hartman, who passed away during the preparation of this manuscript, gave me glimpses of Catherine's zesty spirit, sense of humour and spiritual depth. Marge Denis graciously shared her memories of Catherine.

I am grateful to M.C. Havey, the archivist for the Sisters of Service, for her patient and skillful help during the research phase of the work, as well as for editorial assistance. She and Desmond Wilson, treasurer for the Sisters of Service, were encouraging and supportive, and I miss our lunchtime outings and exciting conversations.

I appreciate the hospitality of those "out west" who helped me to experience Winnipeg, Gimli and Camp Morton, Manitoba. Kay and Herman Ahrens, Sister Mary Gorman, snjm, Wilma Ledingham, Lucy Marks, Rose Reichert and Rev. Arthur Seaman offered insights into the influence of the Sisters of Service in the rural places of the West that Catherine loved so much.

I wish to thank Dr. Jeanne Beck, author of *To Do and To Endure*, the story of Catherine's life, both for her book and for her honesty and sincerity in our discussions regarding Catherine's spirituality. Many people graciously offered gifts of time and expertise, especially Dr. Mark McGowan, Dr. Elizabeth Smyth and Maureen Shave, former principal of Sister Catherine Donnelly Catholic School in Barrie, Ontario. John Burke also read an early draft of the manuscript and offered frank and helpful critique. Gerry McCarthy, and my brother-in-law, Dr. James Haughey, gave me valuable advice when I struggled with the writing process. Paul Gibson, a relative of Catherine's, shared touching stories about her personality and spirit.

Many of the faculty at Regis College, University of Toronto, offered me support, encouragement, guidance and expertise. I especially thank Sister Kathleen McAlpin, RSM, for her friendship, and for the gift of her method of theological reflection, which grounded both my research and my writing. Sister McAlpin, Dr. Margaret Lavin, Fr. Scott Lewis, SJ, and Fr. Michael Kolarcik, SJ, read portions of the manuscript, offering critical feedback and personal insights that deepened and broadened my perspective. My deepest gratitude is offered to Mary Jo Leddy for writing the Introduction at the request of the Sisters of Service. I would like to acknowledge Catherine Mulroney for her work in editing the final draft of the manuscript.

I am grateful for the support of my parents, as well as many family members and friends. Finally, I offer my husband, Alan, and our children, A.J. and Elyse, my most heartfelt gratitude and appreciation for their steadfast love, support and encouragement.

Contents

Sister Catherine Donnelly, SOS: A Chronology

1884   Catherine is born near Alliston, Ontario, on February 26 to Irish-Canadian parents Hugh and Catherine Donnelly, and is baptized at St. Paul's Roman Catholic Church.

1890   Elizabeth Theresa (Tess), Catherine's sister, is born.

1894   Mary Loretto (Mamie), another sister, is born. She later becomes Sr. Justina, CSJ.

1901   Obtains "junior leaving certificate" (Grade 11) at Alliston Public High School and third-class teaching certificate at Model School in Bradford, Ontario.

1902   First teaching position in a one-room schoolhouse at Brandon School No. 10, Adjala Township.

1905   Obtains permanent teaching certificate at Toronto Normal School. Mother dies in November. Father forced to sell family farm.

1906   Moves family into house in Alliston and assumes heavy financial responsibility, including fees for Tess's and Mamie's education.

1907   Begins teaching in rural Ontario schools. Constantly seeks positions with higher pay and greater responsibility. Becomes one of the highest paid teachers in Ontario.

1918   Teaches at Stettler, Alberta. Spanish influenza outbreak. Volunteers to nurse settlers. Experiences vocation to religious life with very specific vision of ministry.

1919   Catherine's father, Hugh Donnelly, dies.

1920   Discusses vocation with Peterborough Sisters of St. Joseph, but is not considered a suitable candidate. Joins Sisters of St. Joseph in Toronto as postulant, but is not accepted into community. Decides to begin new community on advice of, and with assistance of, Toronto Provincial Superior of the Redemptorists, Reverend Arthur Coughlan, C.Ss.R.

1921   With Fr. Coughlan and Archbishop Neil McNeil of Toronto, discusses and plans new community. Returns to Saskatchewan to research conditions and needs. Conceives name "Sisters of Service." Helps choose Sisters of St. Joseph to train first novices.

1922   Sisters of Service officially announced as new Roman Catholic women's religious community. Enters as the first member on August 15. Father George Daly, C.Ss.R., is made official clerical supervisor by Fr. Coughlan. Sister Lidwina, CSJ, is appointed first Novice Mistress.

1923   Wears SOS uniform in public for the first time at 8:00 a.m. Mass on 17 June at Our Lady of Lourdes Church in Toronto.

1924   First vows (renewed yearly until final profession). Rev. George Daly acknowledged as co-founder with Rev. Arthur Coughlan by Archbishop Neil McNeil. Catherine and Sister Catherine Wymbs found first SOS mission at Camp Morton, Manitoba. Catherine appointed to executive committee of Manitoba Teachers' Association.

1926   Superior at Vilna, Alberta. Teaches catechism in rural Manitoba during summers.

1929   Works at religious correspondence at Edmonton Catechetical Correspondence School.

1930   Obtains First Class teaching certificate. Superior at St. Brides School, Alberta.

1933   Catechetical Correspondence School, Edmonton, Alberta. Catechetical tours in Cariboo Mountain region during summer of 1934.

1936   Catechetical Correspondence School in Regina, Saskatchewan. Supervises studies of future SOS teachers. Catechetical tours in Cariboo during summer.

1938   Superior at Marquis, Saskatchewan.

1940   Superior at Sinnett, Saskatchewan. Removed and placed at Edson Mission, listed as "ill."

1943   Delegate to General Chapter of Sisters of Service. A series of teaching positions follow: Diamond Crossing and Jutland in Saskatchewan, Camp Morton, and Regina until 1951.

1949   Silver Jubilee at Mother House in Toronto.

1951   Teaching at Peace River in Alberta and then Rycroft, Alberta.

1956   Rev. George Daly dies. Catherine retires from teaching public school and begins semi-retirement at Camp Morton, Manitoba, tutoring young Sisters.

1964   Catherine's sister Tess dies. Catherine, aged 80 years, passes French course at University of Edmonton.

1974   Golden Jubilee. Receives Papal Medal *Pro Ecclesia et Pontifice*.

1980   CBC's *Man Alive* show features Catherine and Sisters at Camp Morton.

1981   Moves to nursing home in St. Catharines, Ontario. Younger sister, Sr. Justina CSJ, dies.

1983   Catherine dies on 5 September. Funeral at Holy Name Church, Toronto. Rev. C.J. Crusoe presides. Buried in Sisters of Service plot at Mount Hope Cemetery, Toronto.

1990   Sister Catherine Donnelly is officially declared the Foundress of the Sisters of Service by her community, founder of the first Canadian English-speaking Roman Catholic missionary order.

1997   Biography of Catherine Donnelly is published: *To Do and To Endure: The Life of Catherine Donnelly, Sister of Service* by historian Jeanne R. Beck (Toronto: Dundurn Press).

2000   Sister Catherine Donnelly, SOS is named on *The Catholic Register* list of "Top Ten People Who Helped Shape the Church in Canada."

2004   Simcoe Muskoka Catholic School Board names a new Barrie, Ontario, elementary school "Sister Catherine Donnelly Catholic School."

❧ Introduction ❧

"Who is that person?" I asked my mother as we passed by the woman in a grey hat and cape. We were walking on the bridge that spanned the South Saskatchewan River in Saskatoon. It was forty below and bright.

"She's a Sister and she's going out to serve."

"Oh."

As a young Catholic girl growing up in the 1950s, I struggled to understand this new information. I had assumed that all nuns were in convents and they never went out. I thought they all wore long black dresses and covered their heads. In those days, they were all mysteriously different. Or so it seemed.

Later, I would learn that the Sisters of Service, in their simple grey dresses, and with legs, lived in a house by the bridge and that they worked with the poor.

Now I have read this marvellous book and I have understood so much more about the Sisters of Service and their remarkable founder, Catherine Donnelly. I learned why they went out to serve and walked across the bridge to the poor. *The Courage to Dare* tells the story of Catherine Donnelly's pioneering spirit. It is also part of our story, as Catholics and as Canadians.

Who was this person? The following pages reveal a woman who saw things simple and saw them clear. More given to action than words, she set out a pathway for later generations of Catholics to follow.

We read the unfolding story of a young woman from the farmlands around Alliston, Ontario. She went out west to take a teaching position at a rural school in the eastern region of central Alberta. It was there that she saw the immense need of the new immigrants who had moved out onto the prairies to scratch out a living from the land. She saw their impoverished lives and heard the cry of the poor. Yet, she also experienced their capacity for joy and gratitude. More importantly, she was happy to be with them. This was the original experience that would then define her life calling and give her the courage to dare. It was a religious experience that became her vocation to a religious way of life. The meeting of her inner call to the summons of poor immigrant farmers is a concrete example of Frederick Buechner's maxim that "The place where God calls you is the place where your deep joy meets the deep suffering of the world." Catherine Donnelly believed that this call was not only for herself, but for others as well.

It soon became clear to her that she could not respond to the needs of poor immigrants in rural western Canada within the forms of religious life as they existed at that time in the Canadian Catholic Church. She was convinced that the Church had to go out into the world of those who were suffering instead of creating spaces within the Church for those who were suffering. She imagined a religious community of service that did not serve within Catholic schools and hospitals, but rather went out to work in public schools and in remote regions of the prairies.

Thus a new religious community was conceived in response to a need that was not being met by other groups within the Church. This book recounts the many difficulties that Catherine Donnelly encountered as she tried to pour new wine into old wineskins. She had the courage to believe that responding to the needs of those in remote rural areas meant leaving behind structures such as the cloister and a form of obedience that was outmoded. It meant dressing in a more ordinary way so as to be closer to the people the Sisters were sent to serve. Not everyone in the Church understood that the times demanded a new and different response.

As I read this spiritual biography of Catherine Donnelly, I realized that she was one of the mothers of Vatican II, the great Ecumenical Council that gave new shape and spirit to the Church. Vatican II did not drop down from heaven one day. For almost 40 years, in Europe and North America, it had been germinating in the lives of thousands of Catholics. These early mothers and fathers of Vatican II felt their life of faith was bursting at the seams. They became aware that the questions and suffering of the world demanded new ways of living, thinking and praying. These stirrings of the spirit were felt out on the prairies by Catherine Donnelly, and she responded in a daring and courageous way.

It was on the prairies that Catherine Donnelly was called to a new form of religious life that was also a reaffirmation of the fundamental values of radical Christian discipleship. Western Canada is big sky country and its vast and barren beauty summons boldness.

The Canadian economic historian Harold Innis mapped out the difference between the metropolis and hinterland – as it existed in Canada and elsewhere. Catherine Donnelly, as so many prophetic Christians before her, discovered the call of the Gospel in the hinterland. She knew that the Gospel imperative was alive and summoning on the periphery, on the frontier, along the border. She and the Sisters of Service were witnesses to this mysterious reality. She understood that the hinterland was a special place of suffering and joy, life and faith, death and resurrection. The Canadian Church is so much more authentic because of the courageous ones who went out to the hinterland, reminding the centres of political and ecclesial power that there was no privileged place for faith and hope.

Eventually, many of the more traditional religious orders would move outside their cloisters and their ordered lives and would wear more ordinary clothes. Forty years later, her challenge to the Church was heard and acted upon. It has taken some time, and this book, for us to realize how prophetic Catherine Donnelly was.

This book also reveals the great price she paid for such daring prophetic action. She was misunderstood by some in the Church, by some of the people she wanted to serve, and even by some in her own community. The fact that she dared to live out of her strengths as a woman placed her in an inevitable conflict with aspects of the clerical structure in the Church. The path she chose was not always easy or pretty, but it was true.

❧

The Church has changed since Catherine first went out to the hinterlands of Canada. Our country and the world have also changed. The farmlands around Alliston, Ontario, are now the place for gentleman farms and automotive factories. Here, as on the prairies of western Canada, mega-farms have supplanted most of the family farms. With the arrival of the Internet and a multichannel universe, there is hardly any place that can be called rural and remote anymore. Nevertheless, there still exists the stubborn and prophetic refusal to abandon the local realities, whether they be the small neighbourhoods of big cities or the little experiments in sustainable agriculture. The hinterland becomes a state of mind, a place of commitment, more than a geographical location.

Wherever the hinterland is today, Catherine Donnelly reminds us that it is a place that summons faith and hope. She has set us all a good example. In the story of her life, we find the courage to dare in our time and in our place. I am grateful to the Sisters of Service and Kathryn Perry for sharing this splendid story with us.

Mary Jo Leddy
Toronto, 2012

❧ Preface ❧

In 2008, as I was finishing studies at Regis College in Toronto, the Sisters of Service asked if I would be interested in researching and writing on the spirituality of their founder, Sister Catherine Donnelly. I immediately went to the college library and checked out Jeanne Beck's biography, *To Do and To Endure: The Life of Catherine Donnelly, Sister of Service*, to learn just who Catherine was and what she had accomplished. Within a week, I had begun to formulate ideas and methods of approach to such a delicate exploration, along with a certain degree of eagerness and excitement.

As intrigued as I was by Catherine's remarkable story, I was particularly drawn to some of the implications of her vision, insights and proposals for missionary work. I was struck by the prophetic nature of her spirituality, as her suggestions for ministry might easily have come from someone *after* Vatican II – certainly not forty years before! I remain impressed particularly by her insights about spiritual dynamics in community development and education. Her overall vision continues to speak especially to those questioning how to orient themselves as people of ministry and presence in the public institutions that are shared by a diverse population.

My experience working with Sister Kathleen McAlpin, RSM, in her Integration for Ministry seminar at Regis College gave me confidence to answer this call. Her method of theological reflection helped me to engage in the process and offered broad categories under which to organize my research and reflections. Since Sister McAlpin's method places emphasis on the category of *experience*, I believed it would be possible to locate some clues about Catherine's own language of desire within her writings. In these writings I could also get some sense of how Catherine was influenced by her circumstances and her relationship with her own faith tradition, as well as with the faith traditions and spiritualities of others. Through repetitive practice I have learned to trust this process, so I believed it was possible to arrive at some accurate conclusions about Catherine's spirituality. I knew that in many ways I would be arguing for certain interpretations of the data, so I have tried to consider as many angles and perspectives as possible in my attempt to be truthful in my account.

Such a project requires a deeper commitment to knowing Catherine than simply describing facts about her spirituality or outlining a chronology of particular events in her life. This type of research and writing is more like a conversation – there is something dialogical about my relationship with Catherine, even though she is no longer with us. Getting to know another at a spiritual level opens up the most intimate aspects of our shared existence, and invites our own transformation and growth. I knew I would have to be open to this if I wanted to proceed in the research and writing process. I also knew that what I learned and wrote about would have to speak meaningfully to readers today, in our own times of need and opportunity. A key aspect of this work, then, is interpreting Catherine's spirituality for today.

I was intrigued by Catherine from the moment I began reading about her. For example, at the close of a letter to another Sister of Service, Catherine advises her to "face reality and all experience." This seems like simple advice, but is it really? It is profound when considered within the context of Catherine's whole life. She took her experiences seriously, reaching beyond herself to encounter every other particular facet of creation. This orientation kept Catherine alive and alert for the voice of the *other*. At the same time, she dared to speak her own truth in public, discovering her vocation in a place where her deep joy and faith encountered the cries of the poor. Many profound statements punctuate Catherine's letters – succinct, practical communications of wisdom that express much about her own experience of life as a spiritual seeker. Her active life is illustrated by the messy scrawls that often run along the margins of notes jotted down on spare scraps of paper. Within these letters, however, is evidence of Catherine's strong conviction, deep faith and abiding trust in God.

In Catherine I have encountered someone who trusted her own experience of the sacred. Pursuing excellence in her teaching career, Catherine was fully able to integrate work and religious life, finding herself as a member of a religious community yet also placed squarely within the civic life of her beloved Canada. She revelled in daring and she lived courageously. Her often unbounded passion could flare up in anger, just as it could energize her to work herself to exhaustion for the sake of others.

For much of the community's history, Catherine was simply known as the first Sister of Service. Her role in the founding and early development of the Institute was little known among the Sisters who entered the community after Catherine completed her novitiate and left for western Canada. She exercised her leadership by developing the frontier missions imagined in the early vision she shared with Toronto Provincial Superior of the Redemptorists Arthur Coughlan, C.Ss.R., and Archbishop Neil McNeil of Toronto. In the early days of the Institute, Reverend George Daly, C.Ss.R., was appointed to guide and oversee its development. Catherine had no patience for the multitude of official details involved in formally establishing the community, restless as she was to get the practical aspects of the missionary work under way. Because Father Daly had leadership experience, and wrote the original rule for the Institute, and because his understanding enlarged the mission of the Sisters of Service, his influence on the Institute's development was more pronounced than Catherine's. Thus, it was decades later, after the reforms of Vatican II in the 1960s required religious orders to retrieve the spirituality of their founders, that the Sisters of Service came to know more about Catherine's history, her vision and her contribution to founding the Institute.

Catherine left little formal spiritual writing. She held no office within the Institute that would have compelled her to record her prayers, reflections, devotions or spiritual teachings for others. She oriented herself as a Sister among Sisters, sharing in the spiritual life of the community through prayer and work. Her writings reflect this attitude and therefore speak of practical matters related to the activity of the Institute. The Sisters of Service shared a life of common prayer and devotion to God, but Catherine left much unsaid about the particular details of her contemplative life.

This need not serve as a deterrent to seeking some understanding of Catherine's spirituality. Contemporary methods of studying spirituality make it possible to examine the existing material from a variety of angles, interpreting her words and actions as responses to the realities of her context. She would no doubt think this very important. Of one thing I am quite certain. She would frown on idle musings that envision her as a woman whose striving for holiness took her beyond the concrete world. She would expect an energetic and lively study and reflection that acknowledges her spirituality as one person's part in a larger story. She would expect us to be honest, critical, forthright and – above all – ready for change and transformation.

It is a daring project to open another person's spirituality to explanation and analysis, and one that should be approached with profound respect and reverence. It is my hope that in the process of exploring these resources – sharing, praying, reflecting, studying, evaluating, analyzing and searching for insight – a doorway will open into the deeper dimension of Catherine's life. May all who read this book be touched and challenged by her wonderful spirit and come to appreciate its legacy to the Church and the world of our times.

❧ Chapter One ❧

Catherine Donnelly, Founder and Pioneer

I must confess that, though knowing that I ought to have the faith of Abraham, I could not even imagine the astounding things that have advanced our rural Western cause.
And I fear not to say so, and to prove it.

Sister Catherine Donnelly, *Ecumenism Blossoms*

A simple, flat stone in Toronto's Mount Hope Cemetery marks the burial place of Sister Catherine Donnelly, founder of the Sisters of Service (SOS) and a Canadian pioneer in both faith and public service. The SOS community formally recognized Catherine's role in initiating the Institute in 1990, seven years after her death at the age of 99. The honour served as acknowledgement of Catherine's adventurous spirit and determination, which led her to create a new kind of religious community ministering to a vastly underserved part of the Canadian West. That same spirit has both inspired and challenged the SOS to fulfill a mandate of service since the Institute's founding in 1922.

Through her letters and writings, Catherine is revealed as a unique and vibrant woman of faith. SOS members remember her in a variety of ways, never doubting her deep faith in God's providence or her dedication to her religious vocation. From the time of her religious calling in 1918, she devotedly served her Church and country for more than 65 years. For much of her life as a woman religious, however, Catherine's story remained unknown. It was not until her later years that she began to receive recognition and accolades for her contributions both to her Institute and to Canadian society, and much of that focus has come in the years following her death in 1983. These tributes stem, in large part, from the SOS's active attempts to delve deeper into the Institute's history and ethos. After the Church updated its teachings on religious life in 1965, drawing attention to the relationship that exists between the "proper character and function" of each of the Church's institutes and "the spirit and aims" of the founders of those institutes, the SOS made earnest efforts to retrieve details of Catherine's story. The Sisters committed themselves to the admirable and valuable process of retrieval, opening the door to reflect deeply on the spirituality of their founder and their community.

The Vatican officially recognized Catherine's unique contributions to the Canadian Church in 1974, the year of both her Golden Jubilee and her 90th birthday. At that time, George Bernard Cardinal Flahiff presented her with the papal medal *Pro Ecclesia et Pontifice* (for the Church and for the Pontiff), an honour awarded to members of the Church who have offered exceptional service in leadership. In 1980, she was featured in a documentary about the SOS for the CBC's *Man Alive* series and was the focus of Jeanne Beck's biography, *To Do and To Endure*, published in 1997. In 2000, *The Catholic Register* placed Catherine on their list of the top ten people who helped shape the Church in Canada. These accolades all honoured a woman whose life of service spanned much of the 20th century.

Catherine experienced a call to religious life in the fall of 1918, as she nursed poor settlers in Alberta who had been stricken by the Spanish flu pandemic, just as the First World War drew to a close. Catherine and her friend Mary O'Connor had left Ontario to pursue teaching opportunities in the West. Eventually, they found positions as teachers in the small town of Stettler, Alberta, a ranching community located about one hundred kilometres east of Red Deer. Instead of teaching, the two found themselves called to care for the sick after the province's schools were closed to reduce the spread of influenza. As Catherine ministered to the physical ills of the settlers, her eyes were opened to the deep spiritual malaise of her patients and their families. She recognized a situation in need of answers and took her insights to be a gift of God's grace.

When she returned to Toronto, Catherine brought her concerns to Father Arthur Coughlan, C.Ss.R. He was Provincial Superior of the Toronto Province of the Congregation of the Most Holy Redeemer, the congregation commonly known as the Redemptorists. Launching a friendship with that would last until his death in 1943, she began meeting with Father Coughlan at the Redemptorists' provincial head-quarters, adjacent to St. Patrick's Church in downtown Toronto. Father Coughlan soon recognized Catherine as deeply religious, referring to her as possessing "holy desires." She also spoke with Archbishop Neil McNeil, who was likewise troubled by the fate of large numbers of im-migrants flooding into the rural areas of the western provinces. Both men listened to Catherine's concerns and were impressed by her vision. With her cooperation, they began the process of founding the Institute.

Catherine had been particularly struck by her patients' worldly ways. Both she and Mary O'Connor noticed that as soon as those who were suffering recovered their health, their material ambitions also revived. Their brush with death seemed to bring them no nearer to knowing their need for God's help. She spoke about this in *Ecumenism Blossoms*, her memoir of her struggle to found the Sisters of Service:

> There was a strong desire to live and enter the strife again for money, and for comforts, for influence and independence. This was the state of mind, with few exceptions in the homes in both our school districts. We felt that it was general in rural Alberta. The people were not visited by clergy or nuns. Religious work-ers stayed in the cities mostly. Some of the people had been practicing Catholics but the struggle for a home absorbed their

time, and the symbols of religion were out of sight and out of mind. With the light of faith so dim, farm life was losing out.

With the settlers' need as her guide, she interpreted her call as a personal invitation to share in the mission of Christ by planning for some kind of religious life. "It had been a unique experience," she wrote. "It had made me think deeply and feel that I would like to live a religious life."

The path was not an easy one. She had little knowledge of women's religious life in the Catholic Church, as two attempts to join established religious communities were unsuccessful. That experience did, however, help her to evaluate why the Church was unable to respond to these desperate people in the Canadian West. Life in existing communities was strongly shaped by traditional monastic norms unsuitable to her missionary vision. Enclosed within large convents, women religious tended to remain in cities, and few visited rural districts or remote settlement areas. Restrictions on nuns' freedom of movement also made it impossible for them to enter into the kind of work that Catherine was pondering. As well, their manner of dress, their daily routines and the social restrictions placed upon them according to their Holy Rules would not permit them to become the spiritual companions of the settlers in the way Catherine envisioned.

A practical reformer, Catherine proposed a Catholic Institute to complement, rather than replace, these older orders. While she appreciated the work of existing orders, she envisioned something new: a community with a way of life specially suited to the living conditions and specific ministries of the rural missions. As an innovator, Catherine was following in the footsteps of her Irish Catholic forebears – women like Nano Nagle, founder of the Sisters of the Presentation; Mary Aikenhead, founder of the Religious Sisters of Charity; and Catherine McAuley, founder of the Sisters of Mercy. These women had resisted enclosure behind the walls of cloistered convents so as to reach out to those who most needed to encounter and understand God's love and its redeeming power. Each of these women introduced new ways of structuring communities of socially concerned, active religious women.

From the time she and Father Coughlan came to understand that a new religious community was being called forth within the Church, Catherine worked tirelessly to bring this vision to life. She later recalled the earliest days of this realization, saying, "It was only a tiny ray of inspiration overshadowed by a great cloud of indefiniteness." In her world, she saw great opportunity for women to bridge the gap between the Church and society in aid of those most in need. She consistently argued for two pillars to support training for women in religious life: religious formation and professional development.

As religiously devoted women and well-trained professionals, the Sisters of Service were to extend both civic and religious outreach beyond the boundaries of the largely urban middle class – an especially difficult task in the rural context of the sparsely populated prairies. Catherine wanted to encourage faith development for all citizens, regardless of religious background. The members of her religious community would foster and nurture relationships of trust, mutuality, equality and justice. Trust in God and trust in neighbour were mirror images in her spirituality.

Catherine's was the driving vision for the work of the new community, and she was initially offered a place in the administration of the new endeavour. "Probably we shall have some clerical work, etc., in connection with our undertaking for you to do, and His Grace will furnish a desk for you at the Catholic Office Bldg., here on Bond St.," Father Coughlan wrote to her. Catherine, however, desired a role in the mission field. As a model of the kind of missionary Sister she hoped would become the norm for her community, Catherine felt driven to set out for the West as soon as possible to begin putting the plan into action. As a way of coping with the administrative and leadership needs of the new Institute, and with Catherine's full cooperation, Father Coughlan appointed a fellow Redemptorist, Father George Daly, to take up these duties and to get the community under way. As was the norm for new Institutes in the Church, a Sister from an existing order, Sister Lidwina Henry, CSJ, was appointed to oversee the initial formation of the first novices of the new community. Sister Lidwina had been Mother Superior of a CSJ mission in Prince Rupert, British Columbia, for several years prior to her appointment as Novice Mistress to the new Sisters of Service community in Toronto, so she had some experience of life on the western Canadian frontier. Although she had gained some knowledge of the people and the conditions in which they lived, however, her experience was limited, since she and the other sisters set up their convent, with its routines and rules, according to the Holy Rule of the Sisters of St. Joseph. This Rule placed restrictions on their movements and associations with the people of the area, and their daily schedules and activities followed the prescribed pattern familiar to the sisters as cloistered women religious. With some apprehension, Sister Lidwina took on the daunting task of training novices for an entirely new religious community.

Until his death in 1956, Father Daly guided the community spiritually and administratively. He developed its Constitution and Rule, oversaw its financial matters and organized the founding of missions. He guided the spiritual life of the community and the formation of its members. He also enlarged the community's understanding of its particular mission field, moving very quickly to extend the parameters of the field beyond the provinces of western Canada. An energetic promoter of Catholic Missions in Canada, he persuaded the newly founded Catholic Women's League to support the SOS as a way of helping the league forge a national identity. Under Father Daly's guidance, the Institute gradually extended the reach of its missions from coast to coast. He and Catherine agreed on the need and the integrated approach to ministry, focused on both civic and religious development. Father Daly wrote to Archbishop McNeil in 1922 that "[Immigrants] need to be organized not only to preserve and practise their faith, but also to enable them to take their place in the civil life of the nation."

In a very short time, Father Daly, who was directing the quick development of the Institute, was considered in the public mind as its founder. (Father Coughlan's term as Redemptorist Provincial ended in 1928. In 1932, he returned to the United States.) Catherine's role in founding the Institute was soon forgotten. It was only after she began writing to other Sisters, and particularly after Vatican II, that her role in founding the Institute was examined. New members were not told accounts of her early experiences, which had originally determined the mission field and the unique charism of the Institute. Her Sisters regarded her only as the first Sister of Service, but the significance of that initial moment of inspiration in shaping the spirituality of the community was tied to Catherine's unique call to religious life. It was in that experience that the mission of the Sisters first became known, that a particular spirituality was born, that new attitudes were adopted and that a new way of life came into being as an inspired response to God's call.[1]

Catherine's story raises questions about particular features of her spirituality. An understanding of her distinctive spirit can be enhanced by identifying the roots of her religious understanding and by examining how she received and shared her Christian faith. She was not only influenced by others; she also influenced those with whom she came into contact. It is important, therefore, to examine how her faith inspired her to develop creative and innovative forms of ministry as she responded to the needs of the most isolated people in her world. It is also vital to explore how her deeply integrated worldview, an inheritance from her Celtic ancestors, supported her in cultivating a practice of spirituality in nature and in community.

Important aspects of Catherine's spirituality can be discovered by studying her life as a Christian woman, as founder of the SOS, as a missionary and as a minister within the Catholic Church. The following definition by Sister Kathleen McAlpin, RSM, serves as a guide:

> Spirituality is a way of living life from what is believed in faith. A 'spirituality of Christian ministry' is a living response to God and this dream. In living out this spirituality, I believe that those engaged in compassionate ministry are summoned into a process of ongoing conversion. Through this transformation they participate in extending the reign of God, the vision of Jesus for the world.[2]

As McAlpin says, the vision of Jesus is for the world, and it is transforming for both the missionary and for those among whom they minister. Catherine's spirituality took shape as she brought her religious faith into serious engagement with the social and cultural realities of her time. As an educator, she interpreted the signs of the times, listening to the call of the poor to the Church of her day. In deeply imaginative ways, she brought her prayer with Scripture into conversation with her experience. She sought wisdom from Church tradition and teaching, and support from the community of Saints. Catherine believed she was a person uniquely placed by God, capable of receiving inspiration, a person gifted with intelligence and the responsibility to discern her own path of action in faith.

Catherine's image of herself was shaped by her understanding of what it means to be made in the image of God. Beck, in her account of Catherine's life, closes with a statement of Catherine's: "It is extremely important not to separate the spiritual life and the training of the mind. The spiritual life and the intellectual life have the same root deep in the unity of the intelligence." These words identify something essential about Catherine's understanding of the human person, her view of the world, her orientation towards God and her uncluttered way of speaking about spirituality. She proposed a religious mission while remaining grounded in what she called "grassroots reality." She also questioned her Church's understanding about its life in the world, critiquing conventional attitudes and spiritual practices she considered to be outdated or irrelevant, while always seeking to clear pathways into new modes of being Church. Many years after Catherine's death, Pope John Paul II would write, "Faith and reason are like two wings on which the human spirit rises to the contemplation of truth."[3] Catherine worked to ensure that her reason was faithful and that her faith was reasonable.

Catherine's desire was to "get in among the diggers of 'food for the world' and find a way to stay among them." This active spirituality reflected the practical wisdom that emerged from her Christian faith. She was a pioneer in the new socially oriented movements within the Church, and understood the contemplative life as the basis for these active movements. She confronted many prevailing notions of piety and devotion in the Church, especially for women religious. In opening her mind and heart to the plight of the immigrants, she grasped the dehumanizing effects of unrestrained industrialization and urbaniza-tion. She gave voice to the dangers facing farmers and rural dwellers, as social and economic priorities shifted towards industrial and urban development. A woman of great foresight, she argued that these were spiritual concerns that the Church must address.

Through it all, Catherine remained rooted in prayer and compas-sionate solidarity with all people, with nature and, in a special way, with animals. She was passionate, and her zeal for missionary work was acknowledged by all. Courage, bravery, adventure and daring are words that frequently appear in Catherine's writing, often underlined for emphasis. She brought all of her ardour to bear on questions of justice and unity. As Sister Viola Mossey, SOS, recalls, "She was a powerful woman. If she saw a wrong it would concern her greatly and she would want it rectified."

Catherine believed she was participating in what she labelled "a glorious cause." The obstacles and barriers she encountered made her life seem like a quest. She depended on her intelligence and her faith to determine new directions and to make choices. But hopefulness gave way at times to frustration, anger and despair. We honour Catherine when we remember her honesty and consider her painful emotions as part of a whole reflection on her spirituality. In pondering the mysteri-ous ways in which God's plans were thwarted, she would never give the upper hand to evil. It was her willingness to imagine the world anew that brought her to propose revolutionary ideas and methods in her ministry, and this radical openness uniquely shaped her spirituality.

Catherine's story spans close to a century of recent Canadian history. She was an educator, an interpreter of the Bible, an activist, a reformer, a missionary and the founder of a religious Institute. She was a woman whose biography and spirituality offer inspiring insights and challenges for our own times. Hers is a voice well worth retrieving from history, a voice that until fairly recently was in great danger of being lost entirely.

Chapter Two

A Simple Celtic Spirit

God around me, God above me,
God to guide me, God to love me.

Catherine Donnelly's prayer
in times of great need

Catherine described herself as "a simple Celtic spirit." She traced her spirituality back to St. Patrick, a convert to Christianity who became an evangelist to the Irish during the fifth century. Identifying strongly with the Irish because of her ancestral lineage, Catherine kept Ireland in her heart and in her prayers, especially during times when conflict between Catholics and Protestants erupted into violence. Days after fighting broke out between British soldiers and Catholics in January 1969, for example, Catherine wrote to Sister Magdalen (Madge) Barton, SOS, saying, "Pray for Ireland. Dear Ireland! God help them!"

Catherine used the term "Celtic" particularly in reference to the capacity of the human imagination to grasp the artistry of God's creation. One aspect of Celtic spirituality that particularly resonated within her was a love of nature. Catherine witnessed the beauty of nature as an expression of God's grandeur. She was amazed by the marvels of science and astronomy. Grateful for the fertility of the soil and glory of the harvest, she was inspired by the Celtic Christian sense of the world, in which the entirety of creation becomes a sacrament where God can be encountered. In his book *The Music of What Happens: Celtic Spirituality – A View from the Inside*, Father John Ó Ríordáin, C.Ss.R., explains that for those like Catherine who are inspired by this spirit, "everything in nature [is] a reminder of the presence of God; everything [is] a gift of God; everything [is] a revelation of God."[4]

Camp Morton, a small community about eight kilometres from Gimli, Manitoba, along the shores of Lake Winnipeg, was the site of the first Sisters of Service (SOS) mission. Situated one hundred kilometres north of Winnipeg, the area around Camp Morton was first settled in the 1880s by Icelandic immigrants who engaged in lumbering and farming. While these settlers were predominantly Lutherans, another wave of immigrants brought people from the Austrian-Hungarian Empire to the area in the early 1900s, many of whom were Catholics. As a response to the need for a summer camp for Roman Catholic children, the rector of the cathedral in Winnipeg, Monsignor Thomas Morton, for whom the camp was named, bought the property and outfitted it for summer use.

Sister Lena Renaud, SOS, always called Catherine "Sister Donnelly." The two Sisters lived in the house at Camp Morton from 1956 until a short time before Catherine's death in 1983. Sister Renaud, a teacher whose appointment at Camp Morton lasted from 1951 to 1988, got to know Catherine well and spoke often about the older woman's love of nature: "Sister Donnelly expressed much of her spirituality in the great love she had for nature. She saw the Creator in the beauty and songs of the birds, the trees, the animals and all of nature." Because of her recognition of the accessibility of God's presence in the world around her, a practical theology grounded Catherine's practice of faith.

By all accounts, Catherine enjoyed a sense of religious freedom in her early childhood and teen years. As she described it in a letter to Sister Barton, "Through my former experience and, in some ways, underprivileged youth ... I had learned to see Christians who were not Catholics as many of them truly are – more Christian-like than many Catholics are." In the rural areas around Alliston, Catholics and Protestants were about equal in number, and little animosity arose between these groups. Social life developed apace and neighbours lived in amiable proximity to one another. Although life was hard for farmers, Catherine witnessed the natural rhythms of birth, life, death and rebirth that are part of any agricultural setting, and this taught her that new life is possible after hardship, tragedy and loss.

That new life included a fresh start for Irish immigrants, including Catherine's ancestors. In Ireland, most tenant farmers would never own their own farms or be able to pass them on to their children, but prospects were good in Canada. Here, many immigrants found opportunities to imagine a new life. Families became owners of their farms and anticipated a growth in prosperity for future generations. Like many other Irish-Canadian immigrants who settled the rural areas of Ontario, Hugh Donnelly, Catherine's father, had aspirations beyond simply running the family farm. He engaged in some speculation, buying and selling wool from other farmers. Unfortunately, his poor skills at business eventually resulted in heavy mortgaging of the Donnelly farm property and ultimately the loss of the family farm, which was a great blow to Catherine. As a child, she grew up loving the farming way of life and the close-knit community around her Adjala home. Her childhood memories of beautiful rolling hills, family farms and small businesses, as well as her encounter with the diverse population of Simcoe County settlers forever affected her views about social and religious cooperation in rural areas.

Both Protestant and Catholic settlers were able to establish churches for themselves. Catherine's family attended the Church of the Immaculate Conception, which still sits on a hill just above the property where her family's modest farm once stood. Catherine's imagination was shaped by this experience of civic and religious harmony, as well as by the hardships and failures of farm life. Her mother, who was also named Catherine, was a popular woman who was well known in the community. She died of tuberculosis when Catherine was only 21. In addition to this tragedy, her father suffered a series of business failures, but Catherine always regarded her childhood and youth as blessed.

She was able to view the world with all its tensions, its differences and its contradictions, as a *whole* world. Her vivid imagination fired her sense of adventure as she continually reached beyond apparent barriers to discover new possibilities. Her religious faith supported her in good times and bad.

The rural environment, with its community values of tolerance and neighbourliness, had a significant impact on Catherine's spirit. Childhood experiences nourished her deep love of farm life, of friends and neighbours, of nature and animals, of literature and Christian tradition. In these surroundings she developed a strong sense of hope for the future, believing that even though life was full of struggles and hardships, faith made the world a place of opportunity. In her mission among the immigrant settlers of the West, she would draw upon these early foundations to help her inspire others to hope and work for a better future.

Her early experiences of diversity and social cooperation convinced Catherine of the great value of public education. Having attended Ontario's public schools in Adjala Township and Alliston, she later spoke of the benefit of learning in classrooms composed of students of mixed denominational backgrounds. Her formal religious instruction both grounded and complemented what was being learned in school. From her parents – and especially from her mother – Catherine learned about God, prayer, devotion and sacramental preparation. In the busy life of the farm, prayer and work were mutually enhancing activities, and this dynamic would forever characterize her way of life.

Catherine witnessed the fruits of prayer and faith in her mother's integrated practice of religious devotion and social responsibility. She recalled her mother "wonderful, deeply-religious, actively-Christian, self-sacrificing [and] loved by our farm neighbours." She credited her father with inspiring her to responsibly appreciate the gifts of creation, especially with respect to the running of the family farm. These early years were a fertile time for the growth of Catherine's faith in God as she developed confidence in the gift of community. Late in life, Catherine spoke of her desires for her family, expressing hopes that they be "thoroughly good and wisely humble." She felt at home in nature, growing in responsibility and practical wisdom in caring for the world and its creatures.

The culture of Catherine's time was influenced by the rise of the scientific worldview and by the new theories of evolution that were challenging the biblical myths of the origins of life. This shift in attitudes presented both challenges and opportunities. The foundational creation narratives of conventional religious faith were being called into question. Awakened to the beckoning potential of human achievement, people were inspired by this new view of the world and its history. As a result, Catherine witnessed sweeping changes during her lifetime. The car, for instance, replaced the horse and buggy. Medical discoveries promised to eradicate pernicious illnesses and space travel became a reality. Promising advances in science and technology fuelled people's desire to understand humans and their universe by using the tools of scientific investigation. Experimentation in all facets of human experience was becoming accepted as the primary way of knowing the truth about people and their world.

In this rising culture of scientific materialism, faith and religious experience were sometimes either consciously ignored or understood as irrelevant to human progress. Catherine resisted this trend by continuing to value the gifts of her imagination, her faith and her experience of God's mysterious reality. Her resistance was complemented by her love of learning. She embraced new scientific insights and discoveries, and was an avid follower of developments in archaeology, astronomy, science and technology. Paraphrasing Robert Browning to another Sister, she wrote, "A man's reach must be greater than his grasp – or what's a heaven for?" This suggests her conviction that humans must continually strive beyond the familiar to seek knowledge of the new opportunities God is making possible. In a speech delivered to SOS teachers, Catherine quoted Albert Einstein, saying, "Imagination is more important than knowledge." Humans must strive to learn, she believed, but must respect the limits of their understanding and power. This required zeal for learning, along with deep humility and reverence for God, a humility of accepting one's place with respect to God's sovereign authority, and the equality of all neighbours. Although

Catherine was often puzzled by God's ways of working things out, she sought the wisdom of the Holy Spirit to fuel her imagination with new possibilities. She grasped the spiritual value of her encounters with others – especially those in pain, poverty and spiritual aridity. She also accepted the mysteries of pain, suffering and death with faith and deep humility, while constantly striving to learn the ways in which God was reaching out to humans in answer to their needs.

Situating herself squarely in the *story* of God's self-revelation to human beings, Catherine's spirit resonated with the Jesuit practice of seeking God in all things. (In fact, in a piece called "Remarks" concerning the location of the new Motherhouse, Catherine recommended a certain location, saying, "It is near the Jesuits who would accommodate in every way possible, spiritually, and as educational advisors. They are greatly experienced in educational matters.")

For those who, like Catherine, counted their background as Celtic Christian, the story of God's revelation unfolded for the most part in an agricultural milieu. As Father Ó Ríordáin explains, this heritage survives in Celtic Christian attitudes today, reflected in the emphasis on local community and resistance towards bureaucracy and centralized government. Catherine's approach to ministry reflected this ancestral influence. Aware of the need for ministry to be grounded in the personal dynamic of community, she resisted applying general solutions to what were unique and local needs and concerns. Catherine placed confidence in people's capacity for local leadership as well as in her own understanding of the unique challenges facing the establishment of the Church in the West, hurdles which ranged from a shortage of trained professionals to the long distances that prohibited travel during winter months. For Catholics, this meant only periodic visits from a priest. While the SOS would fill a ministerial void, Catherine also envisioned empowering the laity in remote locations to help develop and practise their faith. This became a basic principle of ministry within the SOS.

Catherine's preference for the agrarian way of life over the culture of urban life was an outward expression of her spirituality. She valued life as a farmer, and her encounter with the natural world and its creatures influenced the development of her spirit. She found signs of God's presence at work in the world of growing things, as well as in personal relationships. These were the elements of the world that called to her imagination and shaped her religious sense. Father Ó Ríordáin points out another quality of Celtic spirituality that helps us to understand Catherine's preference for country life: "The Celts opted for simplicity of life with little inclination towards materialism," he writes. "They were the rural people *par excellence*, in harmony with their natural environment."[5] In spite of her father's business failures, Catherine found inspiration in her father's love of horses, farming and the rural way of life. She idealized agrarian traits from her Celtic background, and that influence made the simple, rural life attractive as a place to live her mission.

Celtic Christian spirituality is a fully incarnated spirituality – that is, it takes seriously the fact that God lives among us. Catherine lived in an ongoing relationship with the personal God she encountered in Scripture, in Christian tradition and in the world. She looked for evidence of divine expression within the whole context of the world of nature and society. Because God was *in* her world and *for* her world, she could imagine God's creative and liberating power being revealed before her eyes. Her spirituality professed that personal encounter with Christ opened people to a perpetual fountain of forgiveness for weakness and sin.

Imagination and intelligence were central to Catherine's vision of reform. She remained rooted in practical concerns and basic human development, believing the practical circumstances of human striving were where God's love most mattered. In writing about the trials of her own life, she said, "… with God, I certainly had had a profound training in basic suffering and basic principles." In light of her own experience, she reflected on the situation of the immigrant population and the Church in the West. Her reflections sparked her imagination and sent her in the direction of reform, because of the need for the help of religious women in rural Canada. Naturally curious, and responding compassionately to the real needs of the people she encountered, she was willing to question what most people took for granted. Traditional ways of organizing the religious life of Catholic women were not working, so she suggested innovations. Impediments to the Church's social outreach could be overcome, but a new form of religious life would be necessary. Her spirituality took shape as she strove to embrace and embody this vision. For Catherine, *need* was the primary motivator in her drive for the reform of the traditional religious life of Catholic women. By keeping her focus on the possibility of God's response to those in need, her imagination was freed to consider new ways of coordinating the Church's response.

Catherine's theology and her view of the world exerted strong influence on her spirituality, and her theology was one of *encounter.* This grasp of unity and solidarity could not have developed without some notion of the interrelatedness of all created life. The Celtic Christianity of Catherine's Irish ancestors resisted forms of dualism present in those spiritualities strongly influenced by classical Greek philosophy. In *God Seekers: Twenty Centuries of Christian Spiritualities,* author Richard Schmidt offers this description of the unique characteristics of the Irish people:

> The dualism that saw flesh and spirit as opposed, so prominent among the Mediterranean Christians, found no place among the Celts, who viewed the physical world, including the human body, as the theater in which God discloses himself and therefore as holy. Every planet and star, every rock and stream, every animal and plant, every human being and every part of the human being were subject to divine influence. As a result, Celtic spirituality was immediate, earthy, and intimately bound up with daily living.[6]

As St. Patrick learned in his mission among the Celts, the Christian message resonated in a very distinct way for the Irish people.

The strong sense of being alive within a natural environment suffused with the goodness of God has persisted in the Celtic interpretation of the Christian message. God's presence is encountered as a living force in the natural world and in community. Catherine clearly demonstrated this sense of God's close presence in her exclamation of prayer, "God around me ...." Her prayer is similar in form to a *lorica,* still popularly known as a Breastplate prayer. *Lorica* is the Latin term for a breastplate, and thus suggests the prayer is a type of shield or protection. Consider how similar Catherine's prayer is to that of St. Fursa, from the seventh century: "The arms of God be around my shoulders, the touch of the Holy Spirit upon my head, the sign of Christ's cross upon my forehead." In these types of prayers, the petitioner asks for God's strength, protection and guidance, believing God's power to be palpable and accessible. Catherine's experiences helped her discover that God's presence is encountered as a surplus of spiritual power in the world. As she wrote to Sister Patricia Burke, SOS, "God is standing by – even working miracles." Believing that heaven could be experienced on earth by creatures properly attuned to God's desires, she exclaimed that "what makes Heaven within oneself is to be heading in the right direction." To go in the right direction, in Catherine's mind, was to surrender to the will of God. Life's journey was full of traps and deceptions that could lead people away from what God wanted. Faith was commitment to trusting God and staying close to God's power through prayer and action.

For Catherine, encounter with God was possible in the visible world because the worlds of the supernatural and the natural are in communion. Her conviction that God's presence permeates everyone and everything was at the heart of her desire for human unity and solidarity. This unifying power made it possible to follow Jesus' command to love God and neighbour, overcoming apparent divisions and differences. Catherine staunchly resisted institutions that tried to organize people – especially children – into exclusive groups because of religious difference. All children, she believed, ought to live and learn together as the people of God. Offering advice to two Sisters in 1970, she stated bluntly, "I do not think that organizing Separate (a bad word) Schools is practical in every way. In these times we know that all Christians ought to work together."

As Catherine's faith developed, her spirituality became one of actively and consciously seeking personal encounter with God, neighbour and nature. This approach is at the foundation of her spirituality. God's power was realized in her personal and social experience as well as in nature. God's presence in her world was reality for her, and this meant the divine presence was *personal.* She called upon God as she would a friend, or perhaps an ally, in the face of real human problems. God not only supplied inspiration to act, but also saw projects along. She pointed to evidence, for example, of God's support in the development of the SOS mission: "It has, with God's help, become reality in a big way – even surprisingly." Catherine's prayer life communicated her sense that God was with her, surrounding her with love, keeping her safe, and reminding her to seek what was possible as she went forward. It was her encounter with this personal God that she wanted to share with others.

Catherine's image of God was distinctly Trinitarian; she recognized God as a community of three persons, the traditional way Christians speak about God. St. Patrick, in his famous breastplate prayer, prayed, "I arise today, Through a mighty strength, the invocation of the Trinity, Through a belief in the Threeness, Through confession of the Oneness, Of the Creator of Creation." Reflecting on Catherine's life, Sister Helen Hayes, SOS, noted in her *History of Sister Donnelly*, that the Trinity of Father, Son and Holy Spirit "was the pattern of Sister Donnelly's life, a life filled with wonder and glory." Using certain words and phrases to describe her encounter with the divine, Catherine chose dynamic images of God as ones that were helpful in her active life of ministry. These images of God were discovered and deepened through Scripture, prayer, contemplative life, meditation, action and reflection. At the heart of Catherine's spirituality was her encounter with God, which she talked about in ways that were meaningful and valuable to her and her community.

Biblical spirituality served as a vibrant background for Catherine's theological imagination. While she accepted many of the scriptural ways of naming God used by Christians of her era, notably absent from her writing is any language that speaks of God in ways that evoke fear, shame, harsh judgment or bloodthirsty anger. Hers was a theology of hope and promise. She always viewed human failings within the broader horizon of God's forgiveness and mercy. For those who had faith, there was always opportunity to turn away from sin and to come back to God. As she wrote, "God provides strength against the Evil Spirit."

Her references to God reflected the variety of ways she experienced the sacredness and blessedness of her own life. *Creator* was the image she used to convey her sense that God was the primary reason for her existence as well as her ultimate goal – the *alpha* and *omega* of her life. God placed her within the world, supported her, provided for her needs and protected her from harm. In seeking to know God's will, she sought to know why she had been created as the particular person she was – and therefore what the purpose or goal of her life was to be, according to God's desire. The opening lines of her memoir state, "The story is simple. The Creator plans the time and place and circumstance of His creature's birth and life." In the image of Creator, Catherine found it possible to appreciate the grand story of creation, while encountering God in exciting and personal ways. Referring to a morning of picking berries, for example, she exclaimed, "I love the adventure – a great way to meditate! Not a dull moment if one uses here what the Creator has provided for us."

Catherine's image of the Incarnate Word of God helped her to know Jesus as one who demonstrated complete harmony with the will of the Creator. The divine purpose of Christ was recognized by Catherine in her naming of Jesus as her saviour. Human beings experienced the divinity of Jesus not primarily by acquiring knowledge *about* God, but rather through personal encounter *with* God in Christ. In this encounter, facilitated through Scripture, Christian tradition and the community of believers, human beings experience God as the teacher of what it means to be human.

Catherine believed Christian doctrine only became understandable for people who had first encountered God's love and mercy through experience of community. As she described it in a letter to Sister Hayes in 1978,

> Capable SOS teachers have found excellent ways of teaching Catholic doctrine around where they live without using periods of the daily school program. God provides well for those who

have deep Faith in Him. There is certainly nothing so influential with children as the real presence – a capable sister-teacher right with the children in the classroom. They see her life.

Earlier, she offered this theological insight to Sister Mary Reansbury, SOS, writing in a 1967 letter, "It is not the 'preaching' that is effective but it is the life that an SOS lives among people of all Creeds." At times, she related to Jesus as a master teacher or model. Life's path was adorned with friendships that were the fruit of Christ's love actively lived among Christians. As her lifelong friend Amy Wright, daughter of the Anglican rector in Alliston, recalled, "Our deep friendship would not have lasted all these years unless we had been united in love & worship of our Lord Jesus Christ."

Catherine most commonly spoke of the Holy Spirit as God's communication and guiding influence among creatures. Her relationship with this helper gave her courage in her activities as a missionary, empowerment available in a special way to each member of the community. As she wrote to another Sister, "Your helper will be the Holy Spirit, Himself, and you can be fearless in your desire …." She trusted that God communicated with human beings in powerful ways. Human inspiration, creativity, innovation and understanding were all outcomes of God's communication with those who desired to cooperate in God's work. She advised her community, "We must be brave, daring and trusting in the Holy Spirit. We need to improvise and trust in God's help." The communication of the Holy Spirit helped people discover and understand God's divine intention within the story of their own lives. As she said, "The need for the guidance of the Holy Spirit is plainly seen now by all kinds of concerned people everywhere."

Religiously, Catherine developed along very practical lines; her practice focused on God and was rooted in everyday experience. Encounters with God's presence in the world permeated her thoughts about her relationship with God. She echoed the Wisdom of Solomon in describing God as the author of natural beauty. In her notes for a piece entitled "In the Vicariate of Prince Rupert and the Yukon," for example, Catherine wrote, "The mountains are superb monuments of

God's creation." Describing her reaction to encountering the divine in nature, she wrote, "… it made my heart ache to be with the author of it all." She regarded everything in the natural world – from the protective companionship of her dogs to the wonder of growing things – as signs of God's continued fidelity to his covenant with humans. The sign of Christ's presence was encountered in the compassion and self-sacrificing love of true friendship. Signs of the Holy Spirit were all around her – as help in trouble, revelation of grace, and divine instruction in faith. This rich spirituality animated the life of many Irish Catholic immigrants who arrived in Canada in the early to mid-nineteenth century. We hear its echoes in this expression of the Irish poet Patrick Kavanaugh in *The Great Hunger*:

> These men know God the Father in a tree:
> The Holy Spirit in the rising sap,
> And Christ will be the green leaves that will come.
> At Easter from the sealed and guarded tomb.[7]

Catherine's theology is striking because of her practical approach to bringing her knowledge of God into conversation with the needs and problems, as well as the hopes and joys, of people. She accepted the truth of humanity's encounter with God in faith, living that truth as a matter of fact in her everyday life. This grounded her theology in a practical engagement with God's power and love, truly present and active in human communities.

Catherine's focus remained fixed on the real possibility of divine power rather than on human sin and weakness. She concentrated her attention on what God made possible rather than on her own sins or failings. She was therefore affirmed, late in her vocational life, by Vatican II's emphasis on the essential goodness of creation, writing, "I was inclined to positive approaches to society such as are emphasized today – thanks to Pope John and the Vatican Council." She acknowledged the Christian responsibility to seek conversion, believing that all Christians must work to correct any behaviour that gets in the way of God's love and justice. Noticing that God's plans or designs could be distorted or impaired by the misguided actions of human beings, she named evil, often using bombastic language. Expressing her concerns on the SOS role in schools, for example, she cautioned, "the 'Old Boy' is ever on the job trying to influence clergy, Sisters and others against getting into public schools. Every type of person is his tool if he can try something to defeat the project – to nip it in the bud if possible." But she did not place evil, or the works of the devil, on a par with the intelligible power of divine love. She found evil in human behaviour to be a distortion of God-given intelligence.

In Catherine's writings there is little or no attention given to sin, although there are many mentions of God's forgiveness and mercy. For example, she reflected on the perfection of the Lord's Prayer: "Forgive us our trespasses as we forgive … Forgiveness for all who sinned – who oppose, is indeed in my heart." It is certain, given her dedication to the spiritual exercises, meditations, devotions and common prayers of the faithful, that Catherine understood and acknowledged her sins, but she demonstrated unbounded faith in God's capacity for forgiveness towards those who, like herself, persisted in moving forward to advance the reign of God.

Catherine sought God's assistance and support when urgent questions needed answering. When difficult problems arose, she prayed for God's help so she could learn what God was trying to communicate. She regarded the natural world as a place of learning and revelation – of studying the ways of God. As she wrote, "We in SOS have a very unique charism and God will provide if we stay with it. Follow the Holy Spirit and study to know it!"

Creative, liberating and illuminating images of God speak of Catherine's profound trust in God's constant presence and care. Drawing on her deep love of rural settings, farms, animals and beautiful natural scenes, she opened her imagination to embrace nature as overflowing with spiritual goodness, and regarded St. Francis of Assisi, renowned for his love of animals, as a favourite. She responded to Jesus' practical ways of teaching about God, and in her own teaching she would try to bring the revelation of God in nature to light in the imaginations of her students. Like Jesus, who could use an example as simple as the lilies of the field, Catherine found that resources for religious instruction were always at hand. With her focus fixed on God's persistent call to humanity, Catherine most often spoke of God in active ways. God created, revealed, taught and prompted human beings, luring them forward into more fruitful living.

Her Celtic background shaped her understanding of community and guided the development of her own ideas about missionary work. The notion of community in the worldview of the Celts is distinguished by its personal and interdependent view of human relationships. As Father Ó Ríordáin notes,

> … there is no word in the Irish language for 'private property' and there is no verb 'to possess'. The term for one's property is *'mo chuid'* – my portion; the underlying social and legal position being that the wealth of the community was owned by the community and out of that resource each got enough to live on. It is a concept totally at variance with consumerist values and the cultivation of greed. When Pope Paul VI published his magnificent and revolutionary social document *'Populorum Progressio' (On the Development of Peoples)*, which declared that 'the goods of the world are for the people of the world', I wondered if he had any inkling of the social structure of ancient Ireland.[8]

Both consciously and unconsciously, Catherine endowed the Sisters of Service with many qualities of her Celtic Christian heritage. In a unique way, she merged this dynamic in her own spirituality with St. Paul's teaching about community and the various gifts that cooperate in the Church. She advocated that the Sisters of Service must assume responsibility for the specific mission that had been given to them, while adopting a generous attitude towards other missions within the Church. At all times, she recognized the value of diversity, and that the various religious congregations were united in their dependence upon the same God.

Catherine in 1926 on the steps of the Sisters of Service house
at Camp Morton, Manitoba, their first mission and the mission
where Catherine Donnelly lived for a total of 30 years.

❧ Chapter Three ❧

A Spirituality of Christ-like Service

I have come to serve.

Motto of the Sisters of Service of Canada

From their Institute's inception, members of the Sisters of Service (SOS) have embraced Christ's spirit of service. Fathers Coughlan and Daly, Redemptorist priests, introduced the Sisters to the theology and spirituality of St. Alphonsus, encouraging them to find and serve "the most abandoned." The SOS motto, *I have come to serve*, formally identifies the Sisters with Christ the Servant, who came for all humanity. As the first member of the Institute, Catherine Donnelly brought with her a religious experience grounded in her encounter with God in the person of Jesus, something she had discovered through her relationship with other Christians. Recounting an experience of hospitality during an especially difficult time in her life, she spoke of the encounter opening "a completely new chapter" in her life. She described the experience in glowing terms, noting, "what broadminded, intellectual and loving hospitality in that truly Christian home! No words of mine could fully describe it. God's way!"

At times she spoke about the quality and nature of Jesus' encounters with others, usually when she was trying to illustrate what she meant when speaking of Christian love and justice. Among examples of Christ-like people, she included loving, Christian families, generous settlers on the missions and other missionaries. Remarking on the settlers' gratefulness for the Christian love they encountered among the Sisters of Service, she described the effect these people had on her, or spoke of the way she had been moved by personal encounters.

Catherine's letters describe not only peaceful, harmonious and cooperative relationships, but also encounters with others that resulted in conflict, strife and anger. Her words and actions reveal an ongoing commitment to relationship with Christ and a deep desire to share the blessings of this relationship with others. They also reveal her willingness to act and speak publicly in confronting what she took to be evil or misguided in the social, political, religious and economic systems of her society. In doing so, Catherine demonstrated a full engagement with the political and economic realities of her time and sought to understand them in light of Jesus' message and mission.

Some of Catherine's encounters with others marked turning points in her life as a Christian missionary Sister. In the summers of 1934 and 1936, she and Sister Irene Faye, SOS, embarked on tours through the mountainous regions of British Columbia. They travelled by car, taking only some light camping gear and a supply of resources for catechetical instruction. On this tour, Catherine experienced a type of missionary endeavour that left a lasting impression about the importance of personal encounter in Christian ministry. The two women covered approximately 3,500 kilometres in ten weeks, travelling over roads that were barely maintained, often at great risk. Working with Father A.L. McIntyre, the missionary priest in whose area they were travelling, they visited isolated and lonely homesteaders throughout the vast parish, offering whatever spiritual assistance they could.

Catherine appreciated the people's simplicity of worship and was sympathetic to their needs. She expressed her thoughts in a letter sent to the Motherhouse in 1934 from the mission trail:

No Sunday Mass-service I've ever attended in city church or Cathedral has ever had the effect upon me, that this worship has in the tiny log school with the teacher's desk for an altar. Here at the Mass are the people of simple faith, no matter what the condition of their lives may have been, or are. Their sins are not the sins of the rich and sophisticated. They still believe in God. They have no church. The children have never seen one.

Father McIntyre became an influential model for both Sisters during these trips. Catherine studied his way of being with the settlers and reflected on his likeness to Christ. She praised his respect for the dignity and inclusion of all people in his mission territory. She admired his warmth, patience and empathy towards all, his lively sense of humour, and his willingness to bravely carry on the work of his mission with few resources. Her comments in a piece entitled "The Shepherd of the Cariboo" reveal Father McIntyre's spiritual influence:

> There are none to teach them except the lone Missionary Shepherd who travels constantly and smiles ever and wins the furthest wanderer back to the fold. There could be no closer imitation of the Great Master, human and divine, who travelled over the hills and stayed in the homes of sinners, than a man who labors alone in this vast Parish of ninety thousand square miles, without church buildings or funds or a place to call his home.

The early Rule and Constitutions of the SOS state that the Sisters were to be "like their Master, their divine model." Spiritual formation of the Sisters was ongoing, but Father McIntyre gave Catherine a practical model to emulate in the wilderness context. She believed he embodied many of the qualities of the Master – Jesus of the Scriptures.

Catherine's missionary spirit became even more adventuresome during the exciting trips she took. She relished the challenge of searching to find those most in need of spiritual support, and of befriending people in all conditions and places. She discovered she had the strength and character to endure the loneliness and privation of such missionary work. Sacrificing the comforts of traditional religious life to minister to rural people brought her great joy. Catherine's insistence on being *present* to the poor and abandoned speaks to her practical spirituality and says much about her Christology. Her Christ was the Christ of the ongoing incarnation. She took Jesus' instruction seriously about where to look for Christ: among the hungry, the thirsty, the strangers, those exposed to social embarrassment, those who were excluded from society.

Her experience in the rugged frontiers of the Cariboo, in the remote interior of B.C., highlighted Catherine's flair for such skills as horsemanship and outdoor living. The opportunity to live daringly shaped her identity as a religious woman and influenced the development of her spirituality. Catherine's early experience of adventuring in the Cariboo was a radical encounter with Christ in everyday life, an experience she carried with her as she moved to other missions. As a result, she began to emphasize certain spiritual qualities, finding them to be most significant in the mission of the SOS.

Two of these qualities were especially important. First, Jesus' ministry was one of befriending those who were experiencing obstacles to realizing God's love and concern for them. Catherine's vision was of religious women teaching their neighbours' children, walking with the people in public, listening to them and befriending them in supportive and instructive ways. Second, Jesus actively lived out God's compassion in practical ways, concerning himself with all people, but especially with the poorest and most socially marginalized. Catherine accepted responsibility for compassionately serving the people in rural communities on behalf of the Church. She believed that people who encountered the SOS would encounter the reality of Christ in their midst and respond by becoming active in the mission of Christ themselves. Reflecting on her mission, she said, "It was for women to go among the people – to be with the children all day, during the school year – not just write to the children. 'Go and teach all nations.'"

Catherine consistently explained the simple principles and goals that formed in her mind during the early days of the founding of the Institute. She explained the basic lines along which the rural teaching missions took shape in a letter to Sister Patricia Burke in 1978:

Even in 1920 and before that there was a spirit of ecumenism in Ontario – I experienced it strongly in Northern Ontario, and it was operating in a particular style in the Western Provinces. In the rural areas there were life and death problems for the farmers and other rural workers which needed concentration and common-sense and practical basic skills and no … contest about any brand of Christianity. Laws of the Provinces control the schools and 'pluralism' can be nicely handled by intelligent teachers if they are humble and love all God's children as true Christians ought to do. For all the children, the teacher present in the school with them, loving them, guiding them, was the witness of God's presence and of all things good for them. No work with youth can be more effective – youth who will be the adults of tomorrow.

The principles for the missionary work of the SOS were expressed in the early Rule of the Sisters, and remained a core element of their work. They were to be ecumenical, working in the public sphere of the developing communities and focusing especially on the margins. In the earliest discussions between Catherine and Father Coughlan, the rural public schools, whose development and regulation were overseen by government rather than by religious orders, were to be centres for the Sisters' outreach.

In their spirituality, the SOS embodied the Christian mission of spreading the Gospel of Jesus through their practice of Christ-like love and service. In Catherine's vision, the community would focus especially on children and their families, and then outward to the whole community. She hoped to offer the basics of Christian education within a curriculum that could be fully shared and valued by all Canadian children. This, of course, was based on the then fair assumption that the vast majority of Canadians of her lifetime were Christian, rooted in Scripture and in the basic story grounding all Christian traditions. As she expressed it to Sister Patricia Burke in 1968, "We were to work for nation and Church – the two being a team which must work wholly together if Canada is to be saved as a Christian country."

Catherine's model of mission evokes many themes from Scripture that centre on Jesus' teachings. She often found New Testament phrases an effective way to make her point. In one short paragraph, she referred to "rendering to Caesar," "the labourer being worthy of his wages," and Jesus' command to "Go and teach all nations." Subtler qualities of Jesus' character were also evident in Catherine's approach to ministry. Prominent among these was Catherine's appreciation of Jesus' attentiveness to others. To discern the unique needs facing each community, the Sisters would have to be good listeners. As both qualified teachers and as religious Sisters, they would also be people who could guide, instruct and inspire others in their missions. The key, in Catherine's mind, was respect for the importance of the laity to the Church and a desire to help them take responsibility for their role in advancing the mission of Christ in the world. In Catherine's view, "lay people are the Church."

The story of the disciples on the road to Emmaus, found in the Gospel of Luke, offers a lens through which to reflect on how Catherine linked Jesus' way of being with others with the mission of the SOS. In this post-Resurrection passage, two of Jesus' disciples are leaving Jerusalem, walking along the road to the town of Emmaus. As they travel, the risen Jesus, whose identity is mysteriously hidden from them, joins them and asks what they are discussing. Amazed that he does not know what has been happening, they inform him of the events of the crucifixion of Jesus, the missing body and the women's reports of Jesus' resurrection. The two are obviously confused about the meaning of these events.

As Luke then narrates, Jesus begins to "open the scriptures" to them. He helps them to relate the meaning of the events to what has been written about God in their own sacred writings. As the discussion unfolds, the stranger is invited to share a meal with the disciples. Jesus takes bread and blesses it, and the disciples realize who is in their midst. With that, Jesus disappears from their sight. They recall that as they listened to Jesus they were transformed, and their despair gives way to enthusiasm, prompting them to return to Jerusalem. In Christian tradition, this story has long symbolized the change of heart and mind that is *conversion* to the message of the Gospel of the Risen Christ.

Modern readers approach this story with an understanding that the stranger on the road is the risen Christ, even though he appears to the two disciples as an ordinary traveller, presumably clothed appropriately for a journey. Catherine's insistence on inconspicuous dress was linked to her image of Jesus as she encountered him in Scripture, practically moving about among the people and performing good works. Before Vatican II's reforms in the 1960s, most women religious wore habits, which heightened their visibility in the broader community and served as symbols of their commitment to a monastic lifestyle. Socially, that lifestyle limited women's interactions with others and lent them an air of *separateness*, setting them apart from existence in the so-called profane realm of ordinary society. Catherine believed those forms of dress and lifestyle were obstacles that kept existing orders from con-necting with the people in their societies, especially with those who were not Catholic. In *Ecumenism Blossoms*, Catherine stressed that she "had a strong 'prejudice' or logical feeling about the cumbersome clothing and the Customs of nuns." She goes on, "I felt that charitable, effective work among the abandoned did not depend on copying the quaint, obstructive, and anti-approachable dress worn by so many good women." Writing to Sister Agnes Dwyer, SOS, in 1962, she implied that the medieval style of dress of the traditional orders was connected with escapism, stating that she envisioned women, inconspicuously dressed, "following the Master as far as humility, meekness, courage and endurance are concerned …."

For Catherine, serving in the name of Jesus meant listening for what people needed most and working to bring God's love and justice to life in the community. She often linked the words *need* and *feasibility* in her writing. She wanted to foster attitudes of trust and gratefulness, focus-ing on what God was doing in the midst of a community. As Jesus did with the two travellers, she wanted to help people interpret the Word of God for their own times and places. The wisdom of Scripture, the religious and moral teachings of the Church and the practical help of the Sisters were to guide people who faced particular problems and crises. The best way to begin was to seek a genuine encounter with the people where they lived. This happened in quite ordinary ways in Catherine's life as a rural teacher. By listening to the little ones in her classrooms, she heard a great deal about what the settlers needed. Visiting their homes and teaching their children catechism gave her opportunities to meet families and hear their stories. She listened keenly to the desires of the students. When a group of young girls said they wanted to study chemistry so they could take nursing, for example, she immediately began to provide what they needed, including the proper classroom supplies.

Catherine's approach to learning the needs of her students also helped her to identify their spiritual needs. This model of missionary work is quite different from one in which the missionary comes with a predetermined program, already certain of what must be taught. Catherine's concern for the responsibility of Catholics to participate in the construction of their societies as moral, rational and religious subjects is striking, especially considering that the Church's social teaching was still grappling with the questions arising from the modern understanding of the human individual and the corporate social order. Beginning in 1891, with Pope Leo XIII's encyclical *Rerum Novarum* (On Capital and Labour), the Church began expressing concern about just social order, which has continued with the issuing of encyclicals on the subject until the present. Catherine's approach to social justice was practical, rooted in the real needs of people and their social rights, but also stressed the responsibility of people for building social structures. Catherine understood the importance of seeking to understand the perspectives of the people she wanted to help. She depended on them to help by giving her information about their lives. She asked questions, and she listened, both as a teacher and a religious worker.

In the story of Jesus and the two disciples on the road to Emmaus after the resurrection (Luke 24:13-35), Jesus walks with the travellers in a companionable way. In a similar style, Catherine did not walk ahead or behind the people she served, but at their side. She showed interest in the events and struggles of their lives because she knew that within the people themselves – and especially the children – there was a capacity for recognizing what was good and of God. As she told Bishop Henri Routhier, OMI, a member of the hierarchy who was interested in her ideas and with whom she communicated frequently for many years, "the Church grows wholesomely and surely through the rural children. We must be daring and feel quite sure of God's help." Ideally, this attitude is at the heart of all Catholic missionary work, but history has taught us that not all Catholic missionary attitudes convey deep and abiding respect for the unique religious experience of others. Catholic missionaries have not always taken appropriate measures to learn about social, political, cultural and economic realities in their mission territories – a danger Catherine pointed out to her own community.

Luke's account demonstrates how Jesus helped the disciples understand the meaning of their own Scriptures in a different way – a way that helped them in a time of crisis. The Church that follows Christ is therefore a community that must always interpret Scripture and traditional teaching anew in the face of contemporary challenges and possibilities. Jesus opened the Scriptures by explaining the relevance of God's ongoing relationship with them in the events the disciples were experiencing. He invited them to consider the mysterious ways God had been at work, and the kind of power they had witnessed in the one whom they had followed. He encountered people in their sense of being lost: they had not been able to find meaning in what had happened and they had lost hope. Their encounter with him opened their eyes to appreciate that the mission was far from over.

Catherine's desire was to enter discreetly into various communities in the name of Christ. She wanted to walk side by side with people, helping them to remember the traditions of their heritage and to know their true value and meaning. She wanted to invite people in quiet ways to deepen their relationship with the sacred, with Scripture and with their faith community through their encounters with Christ. Beyond this, she hoped to assist and encourage Catholics to participate in building their country, confident that their unique gifts of faith were needed as part of Canada's social development.

Catherine proposed that SOS missionary women model the way Jesus came to his own people. "Our dear Lord went into the homes of sinners – and not just for a few summer weeks – He lived among them,". she stressed. She emphasized the humanity of Jesus without denying his divinity. Jesus lived a fully human life as a person who *needed* to know, *needed* to eat, and *needed* a place to stay. Fully divine, he still required the necessities of life. The SOS therefore came closest to modelling Jesus when they arrived as humble members of the community, fully expecting to share in the responsibility of community life. Reflecting their experience of Christ, early Christian communities strove to develop equality, mutuality and solidarity among their members. Likewise, SOS members lived among the poor and shared what little they had with their neighbours. They graciously received what their neighbours were able to share with them. Poverty and humility were conditions of the spiritual life that helped orient the SOS towards those who needed their help the most. As Blessed Teresa of Calcutta would later teach to an appreciative world audience, it is human encounter that makes knowledge of Christ possible.

As a teacher, Catherine's experience taught her that the public school was a good hub around which to build community, presenting favourable conditions for missionary work. Catherine always insisted that as teachers, the Sisters needed to live as Christians among the people – right among them, shoulder to shoulder, because good teach-ers can evoke the compassion of the community, joy in the children's accomplishments, and a sense of hope for the future. A letter to Sister Patricia Burke in 1979 is indicative of Catherine's many comments about living among the people. In the correspondence, she mentions that the Sisters gain their "experience at ground-level, and in the midst of the people, where reality can be seen by the human workers." One of the aims of the SOS missionary project was for settlers to discover their own capacity for generosity, gratitude, compassion and mercy. This active spirituality would empower them to integrate their faith and civic responsibility in a promising new country. Society can be reshaped when people come to discover virtue within themselves and others. Encountering the SOS, people observed that the Sisters brought a very new kind of order with them through their spirituality of ministry in the companionship of Christ.

Like all Christians, Catherine asked herself the question Jesus posed about his identity: "Who do you say that I am?" The titles she used for Jesus were common for her time: Master, Teacher and Lord, names that describe Jesus as a supreme leader and teacher. As a fully human person with a divine mission, he helped his followers learn how to cooperate with the reign of God on earth that was being inaugurated through him. To Catherine, Jesus revealed that God's compassion is expressed in Jesus' suffering with humanity. The Latin roots of the word compassion are *com*, which means "together" or "with," and *pati*, which means "to suffer." To live compassion in the way Catherine envisioned required a great deal of mutual support, and that meant living in a community of people who shared this mission. Catherine's community was to be Christ-like – humble and grateful for opportunities to live actively and compassionately among the poor and most abandoned. This attitude allowed Catherine to develop a distinctive approach to the problems of Catholics in the West.

In her mind, compassion was the most obvious quality of the energy God provides to fuel the constructive work of people. She believed that when people live compassionately, they reveal God's goodness at work in the world, and she had proof. "It is the kindness of the Sisters, their generosity and resourcefulness with poor or afflicted people, their interest in every child, that have really influenced the people and drawn them towards the Church," Catherine wrote. While she did not deny that people are easily persuaded towards evil, she believed that people of faith are attracted to lives of compassion and truth. From the earliest moments of Catherine's vocation, she was drawn to notice the plight of the poorest and most abandoned settlers in the West. It was only after her encounter with them, and only after the movement of her heart called her attention to their need, that she thought of the event as a call to religious life. The compassion she discovered within herself, she believed, had its source in God's compassion for all.

Catherine always spoke of divine compassion as a quality of love that must be lived and encountered in practical ways. She trusted that the fruits of personal encounter with God's love would eventually be realized in the concrete life of the community: "God can Build the

House. Slogans will not build it. Preaching out to the open spaces will not build it. It must be done by living among the rural people," she advised. Others, meanwhile, saw Catherine as extending herself in the service of Christ through extreme measures to reach the most abandoned. Father Coughlan acknowledged she had thrown caution to the wind in her desire "to help abandoned souls and gain them for Christ!" Her motivation came from her understanding of the care and concern God wanted to express to humanity through a unified Christian Church, rather than from any desire to promote the truth of Catholicism over other Christian denominations. "You know our technique is quite something different to that of other Sisters," she wrote Sister Barton. "We get into a school and win, not by talk or acting as if we were something 'right' when all others [are] wrong or by pushing for one Christianity system alone. Let all other Christians have a chance – be fair to all." Her active life of following Jesus in teaching, guiding, leading, serving and befriending the settlers in the West was grounded in the image of Jesus as God's compassion for the world.

Theologian Monika Hellwig articulates what lies at the heart of Catherine's Christology when she notes that "the primary source for Christology is the historical and risen Jesus as experienced and testified by the community of believers from the beginning."[9] Catherine spoke about Jesus as the truth of the risen Christ she had encountered in communities, and she found the image of the risen Christ to be most appropriate to the mission field. God's compassion for humanity was expressed in Jesus' triumph over death and despair, an image that could offer inspiration and hope to settlers in the hard struggles they faced as farmers in the West.

Once the Sisters left rural communities, Catherine knew reminders of their presence would be important. What would be cherished would be personal encounters with the SOS community: the picnics, the celebrations of Baptism, First Communion and Confirmation, and having the Sisters as guests in their homes. Those memories were captured in photographs and written about in *The Field at Home*, the Institute's quarterly magazine. The settlers did not come to have faith primarily through learning facts or ideas about God. Their faith grew through their encounter with God's love in the midst of their daily lives. When Catherine encountered people who had forgotten – or had never known – this God of compassion and mercy, she was prompted to carry the good news of God's love to them because they needed it. All the Sisters knew their time among the people could be short. If a lasting Christian community was to develop, the presence of the risen Christ must remain among them as the active power of compassion and justice. Settlers would have to discover God's presence in their encounters with one another and within the new world in which they now lived.

Given her philosophy regarding the role of teachers as community and spiritual leaders, Catherine was always disappointed that so few teachers joined the SOS. She believed people needed spiritual leaders, guides and companions as they learned how to put their faith into action. She argued that the women of the SOS must be physically present among the people, even though it was God whose power was the source of community development. Describing clearly what she meant, she tried to establish a method for missionary work that respected people's need to encounter God: "Go and teach all nations does not mean live in a city house and teach them by 'remote control.' There is only one way to thus reach abandoned rural people and we have found the way – through the public schools."

Catherine confidently analyzed Scripture in light of her own questions and concerns. In this interpretation of Jesus' ministry, she emphasized Jesus' *personal encounter* with the marginalized in his time on earth. She took this to be a fundamental principle of Christian mission. She believed formation of the SOS should take place along the lines of personal presence and social involvement. In this way she tied their mission closely to that of Christ, a connection made clear in the Institute's chosen motto. Reflecting on the ministry of Jesus, Catherine listed qualities she tried to develop according to his example: "Humility, meekness, courage and endurance." She admired these traits in others, especially when she encountered them in the Sisters of her own Institute. Describing Sister Lena Renaud of her community, for example, Catherine wrote about the qualities of kindness and devotion, adding, "Her humility and Christianity-in-action, her selfless daily life – these are what bring people closer to God."

As a founder, her approach to ministry and mission was practical, and her spirituality reflected this. Although she was well acquainted with Catholic doctrine, her own encounters with people in real-life settings guided her learning concerning the place of Christ in her own spirituality. In *Ecumenism Blossoms*, as well as in many of her letters and notes, she talks about the care and compassion she witnessed in people, describing them as Christ-like or true Christians. These were opportunities to point to the presence of Christ in those of other denominations – not just to make a point about unity, but to witness to those Christ-like qualities of compassion and love she had encountered in these people. These encounters convinced her of the importance of *presence* and *encounter* in her own relationship with God. Her choice to develop a religious life in public, rather than in the enclosed convent, speaks of her desire to foster this spirituality in her community. She did not wish to be present simply to convey certain information about God, but instead to enliven the dynamic of human interaction and guide it in the way of Christ.

Catherine placed emphasis on the affective life of humans – that is, the life of the senses, feelings and emotions. Likewise, she wanted to develop mature Christian communities where people lived intelligently and reasonably. Success, she wrote, would come "through getting among people, being mature in our approach, mature in all our efforts, and working in peace and unity." As she never tired of repeating, the Sisters needed to live among the people to fulfill their mission of Christ-like service. Her statements about Christ-like people focused on their capacity for compassion, generosity, mercy and love – lived out in concrete ways with other people.

One of the great influences on Catherine's ecumenical approach, as well as her understanding of Christ-like love, was the MacDonnell family, Baptist friends with whom she had boarded while working in Galt, Ontario. They had moved to Park Road in Toronto; Catherine turned to them for support and comfort in 1920 after she received the devastating news she would not be proceeding to the novitiate of the Sisters of St. Joseph of Toronto. Later, she recalled in *Ecumenism Blossoms* how she was received by these devout friends:

> I was made to feel that I was loved and trusted, valued as one of the family, and most welcome in this high-class family, which honored Jew and Gentile. My loving Creator who had chosen for me a life of many deprivations, had more than compensated by providing for me in His own unique way, along life's hard road, some of the very lovliest (sic) characters possible to be my loyal, helpful friends.

To Catherine, the MacDonnells demonstrated the kind of love followers of Christ offer others when they truly know Christ through Scripture, tradition and community. The MacDonnell family did not focus on intellectual debate about what had happened. Nor did they moralize about what had happened to Catherine. They respected the deep spiritual discernment process in which she had been engaged, and Catherine valued their love and trust, as well as their willingness to include her in their family home. She appreciated their sense of true welcome, which took her distinctiveness into consideration. In the MacDonnells, she found true mutuality in the respect they showed for her. She also found friendship. Catherine would later cite these qualities as essential to the mission of the SOS in the West. For her, they would always be a sign of the imitation of Christ, a reason to advocate for ecumenical attitudes among Roman Catholics.

While Catherine appreciated the human characteristics of Christ, a photocopied page from the February 10, 1975, edition of *Time* magazine, entitled "The Hartford Heresies," reveals she was also interested in the theological challenge of answering the question "Who do you say that I am?" from the perspective of Jesus' divine transcendence. She wondered how Christology influenced the social justice work of the Church in society. Without a Christological foundation, would Catholic action for justice be any different from other forms of social work? She underlined and bracketed the following quote: "Christianity will be too weak for sustained attack on social evils – or for anything else – unless it first seeks the transcendence, power and will of God."

Catherine connected the Jesus of Scripture with the compassion of her Christian friends, demonstrating her appreciation for God's concern lived out among neighbours. But as for the source of that compassion, Catherine believed Jesus perfectly demonstrated God's compassionate love for us. That compassion, with its source in the eternal love of God, makes human love and justice possible. If it is correct to say Catherine encountered Jesus as the revelation of God's compassion, then her desire to become Christ-like would be a desire to both give and receive the compassion of God. Jesus expressed God's compassion in practical ways among the poor, and Catherine drew upon the same fountain of divine compassion as the motivating power for her ministry because, in his everyday interactions with others, Jesus presented himself as a person who opened people's awareness to the possibilities of God's reign. He used parables like The Good Samaritan to teach that all people are able to both receive and give the gift of compassion, since all are children of the same God. Jesus received the love of others without shame. He was not ashamed to ask a Samaritan woman for a drink of water, or to allow a woman who stepped beyond the bounds of propriety to anoint his feet. This was the unparalleled powerful model Catherine and the SOS chose to emulate.

After his death and resurrection, Jesus' compassion was remembered in Christian communities and their actions are recorded in the New Testament. Catherine lived out this memory of, and witness to, Christ in her spirituality by embracing the gift of her poverty. The basic needs of the Sisters prompted genuine compassion in others, who came to share their food and to offer the things they needed to live in their mission houses. Catherine's numerous accounts of the generosity of the people were intended as witness accounts to the growth in Christian community. They reveal her belief that the true raw materials of Christian community are to be found in the qualities modeled by Christ. She became animated when describing the progress of the community, but rather than focusing on the numbers of children who received catechism or sacramental preparation, she talked about the generosity, compassion, sincerity and trust of those who helped the Sisters to serve them. These, for Catherine, were the qualities of development in which she took most pleasure and which sustained her hope.

Since Catherine's concern was to help immigrants successfully integrate themselves in Canadian society, she refused to engage in any form of proselytizing. She believed such an approach would lead to group enclosure, creating division and hostility among community members as a whole. Throughout its history, the SOS has consistently demonstrated this attitude towards other denominations and religions. Catherine's belief in God's concern for all was reinforced each time she encountered tolerant and friendly citizens working together for the common good. She believed it was possible to develop communities of Christian friendship across denominational boundaries. Christianity began in realizing the essential unity in which people actually lived. Catherine hoped that when people realized they needed one another's gifts and abilities to survive the harsh conditions of the prairies, they would seek unity rather than division.

Catherine's goal was to develop communities who lived Jesus' way of compassionate mutuality. Jesus risked living in relationship with those on the margins of society to demonstrate compassion in very public ways. He advised those who would come after him they must search for him among the poor and destitute – in other words, they must seek him in acts of mercy and compassion. Followers of Christ must always move beyond the safe places and groups in society if they wish to identify with those in need, and that means there is always an element of risk when entering into relationship with those abandoned and forgotten by society.

At turning points in her life, when Christian love became the answer to her own needs, Catherine encountered Christ-like love as the practical expression of compassion. For example, she described the way she felt at one particularly hard time in her life: "utterly sick at heart, trampled in the dirt, completely friendless and despised." She knew what it was like to be rejected, but she also knew the vital power of Christian love. When people reached out to her in Christ-like ways, she believed she was encountering God's compassion through their actions. Like Paul, she encountered Christ as the visible image of the invisible God (Colossians 1:15). Following Jesus meant wanting contact with people so they could experience, via the encounter, the love God had for them.

Catherine believed that as Christians discovered their capacity for compassion and began to experience its fruits in their lives together, they would gain confidence in expressing their faith in the public realm. Since compassion was at the heart of this, the dangers of division and hostility would be less likely to arise. Instead, Christians could discover shared aspects of their faith and help each other build a united nation. This was Catherine's understanding of true ecumenism. She believed that since the power of Christ's compassion comes from God, the possibilities of ecumenical action likewise are made possible by accepting God's gift of unity in a spirit of compassion, as Christ truly did and does.

❧ Chapter Four ❧

A Biblical Spirituality – God Provides!

The dwelling place of God is with men.

Revelation 21:3, underlined in Catherine's Bible

Catherine Donnelly believed the initiative for religious activity rested with God – that God was transforming the world and that she had been invited to participate in this ongoing re-creation. This was the spirit shared by all who participated in the founding and subsequent growth of the Sisters of Service (SOS). In 1937, Father Daly wrote to Sister Margaret Guest, SOS, at the time of her election as Sister General, "My first and most important recommendation is to place your trust in Providence. It is God's work – the work of the Church, you are called to do." Catherine likewise placed her trust in God's provision for the Institute. Writing to Sister Mary Reansbury in 1966, she said, "There is no set way for SOS to get into Public schools which are their right kind – their 'mandate' their unique field. God provides different ways." Catherine's expression illustrated her belief that God was providing for the work of the Church *in* the world – a project of transforming the culture from within social institutions shared by all. This required constant discernment. It is a spirituality that was and is the lived expression of the SOS.

In the biblical spirituality so embraced by Catherine, attention rests on God's activity. The human quest for God is considered in light of God's creative and redeeming power. Religious seekers attend to what is being revealed in the history of the world to know God and to deepen faith. The influence of biblical spirituality on Catherine meant her focus remained fixed on the apostolic work to which she and the SOS had been called. The theme of forgetting herself in the active service of God was grounded in her biblical theology and was foundational in the spiritual formation of all the Sisters of Service. Self-forgetfulness, in this sense, is born of trust in God's providence.

For Catherine, Scripture was a sacred encounter with the God of history, full of relevant meaning in the struggles of everyday life. Its stories spoke about those who had walked before her in history, both trusting and failing to trust in God's steadfast commitment to human beings. These characters became the examples, models and guides Catherine incorporated into her approach to helping others. In attempting to help one young man who was particularly destitute and in need of both material and spiritual help, for example, Catherine pondered the parable of the Good Samaritan, explaining, "I cannot in conscience be one who 'passes by.'" The enduring message of Scripture rested upon God's steadfast presence and faithful provision for creation.

Catherine was inspired by Abraham's story, as he learned to trust in the truth of God's sustaining and life-giving power and in God's real interest and concern for humans. Her patron, St. Paul, was the prototype of the socially engaged Christian missionary – an example of trust in God, apostolic zeal, self-sacrifice and courageous commitment. Catherine desired her life to be one that continued on the path of the biblical saga. At times, she echoed Paul, writing to Sister Patricia Burke, for example, that "Catherine Donnelly happened to be the one who pioneered in outlying places – not because she was worthy of this privilege but because it was God's will." (Paul speaks in 1 Corinthians 15:10 of his unworthiness to be called an apostle, adding, "But by the grace of God I am what I am, and his grace toward me has not been in vain.")

Encounter with the God of history in contemporary life was at the heart of Catherine's spirituality. At different points in her life as a Sister of Service, she spoke about a personal experience that became a turning point in her life. From the moment she dared to ask how she might respond to the flu victims of 1918, she was grasped by concern for them. She began to consider their needs in light of the Gospel mission. God's call moved Catherine's heart with concern for others and sparked her religious imagination. The biblical roots of her Christian spirituality inspired her to conceive of God as the divine power who responds to the needs of human beings. If the prayers of human beings sought God's help, she trusted that help would be near at hand. She viewed the world both as the place where God is to be found and as the object of God's saving love.

Catherine trusted in God's steadfast love and provision, believing this trust bore special fruit in the lives of those who conform to God's will. She shared her concerns and hopes with Sister Madge Barton, a pioneer SOS teacher and catechist who had joined the community in 1927 and who worked as an SOS in western Canada for over 45 years. Knowing that Sister Barton truly understood the needs of the people in the West, Catherine wrote to her about her keen sense of responsibility for the direction of the community and her faith that God would provide what was needed to see her original vision become reality, saying, "But I can only talk and explain – and leave it up to God to do the rest. Whatever is God's will is the thing to do. The open spaces of the Western provinces need us more than ever."

Like Paul, she focused on the reality of God's power and wisdom breaking into the world. Trusting in God's help, Catherine courageously reached beyond the boundaries of social norms for women of her time – both lay and religious – to engage in missionary work. Her willingness to take great risks was legendary among those who knew her; she embarked on daring new projects, overcame obstacles and bravely set out on journeys into new frontiers. Commenting on her stamina, Father Coughlan observed,

... you seem to be always sent to the front lines, perhaps a better word for it would be trenches – but that is your fault, you are always so willing and capable for pioneering that the Superiors, when a rough and difficult assignment confronts them choose you for the clearing of the wilderness.

For Catherine, God intended to teach her through the joys and struggles of her life. "God has provided me with circumstances which educated me along certain lines," she wrote. Some hard circumstances had indeed challenged her faith, but she believed earlier struggles had prepared her to undertake a radical and ecumenical mission in her religious life. Writing to Sister Agnes Dwyer in 1965, she said:

My dear old Father died in Dec. 1919. It was a terrific problem for me for years before that to earn enough constantly teaching wherever I could get the most salary to keep my two Sisters going along with their studies. I should have been doing more for my father too. The challenge was really too much for my ability I suppose or perhaps for my faith in God's help.

The experience at times seemed cruel, but it taught me many things. Necessity does it – what nothing else would do. I found true Christianity among non-Catholics whom I contacted. I found the fairest attitude from Protestant School Boards. I was alone in the planning of my struggle for me and mine and learned to see the truth.

Although life's lessons were sometimes painful, necessity drove Catherine to seek creative solutions. When answers came to mind, she attributed them to the inspiration of the Holy Spirit. "Through using our God-given talents and energy, the Holy Spirit works in dedicated people – Action a thousand times as much as words," she said. When she encountered true love, compassion and mercy in others she acknowledged the presence of the living God at work in these friendships and professional relationships.

Scripture strongly influenced Catherine's reflections on her experience. Her letters and writings were punctuated by many references to both Old and New Testaments. In a more subtle way, biblical patterns and themes were woven throughout her words – themes relating to the saving work of God in history. The truth Catherine encountered in Scripture was a living and dynamic force in her life. She believed the Church could grasp this truth in ever deeper ways by seeking to know it as an answer to the urgent needs of human beings. "The Church continues to grow in understanding of Scripture," she wrote to another Sister. "The truth should not be feared. The Church is not static. The Scriptures are an area where most of us are ignorant. But human genius like yours is seeking to know more about God in His Word."

Seeking to know more about God in his Word, for Catherine, meant that the Bible's eternal truth must be interpreted anew by each generation of the faithful. Remaining close to Scripture was necessary for hearing the Word of God in her own time and place. The traditional practice of *lectio divina* in Christian tradition is the practice of listening with a prayerful attitude to God's Word. Catherine's relationship with Scripture was prayerful and attentive, and she listened to God's Word to better understand what God was asking of her in her own unique time.

Catherine hoped to share the spiritual gifts she had received through listening to the Word of God in Scripture. She was convinced Bible study could be fruitful in the schools if introduced by Sisters trained in its proper use in prayer and reflection. As she noted, "I have always advocated a prepared and skilful use of the short period every morning used for the Lord's Prayer and the reading of the Bible." She knew encounter with God's Word was an essential dimension of her faith development. Reading the Bible provided relevant spiritual insights leading to effective action. Concerned always with the practical needs of humanity, she kept up with news of developments in the world, trying to understand them in light of her faith. At the time of Vatican II, she spoke of her desire to connect the development of reason with the gift of biblical inspiration, she noted, "Far too long did Catholics have outmoded thought patterns and the reading of the Bible is still uncommon." She knew that a revival of biblical study was influencing theological thought and wanted Catholics to be influenced and reinvigorated by the new ways of understanding the Christian mission.

For Catherine, the Bible held within its covers something like an account of humanity's relationship with God. Its stories, phrases, images, aphorisms and pithy wisdom statements helped her interpret her experience of God, and its meaning in her present circumstances. From the creation narratives onward, the story of God's relationship with people helped her to accept the unity of all creation under God's care. She used biblical phrases and referred to biblical stories and characters to communicate religious ideas to other people in her community, finding parallels, for example, between biblical accounts of Abraham's journey in the wilderness and the life of missionaries in the remote settlements of the West. Abraham, Sarah and their descendants lived as wanderers, always distinguished by their difference and always living on the margins of society. She expressed that the plan of the SOS was that they should "act in a peripheral way" and that they "have a spirit quite distinct." Speaking of the faith of Abraham was a dynamic way for Catherine to highlight the Sisters' willingness to travel and live in remote and sparsely populated areas. While attending to the missions, the Sisters made friends with as many of the local residents as possible. Often they found themselves doing missionary work among people whose language, religious background and way of life were not familiar to them.

Catherine consistently focused on the novelty of what God was making possible in the Church's response to new challenges. The use of the public schools as bases for the development of Christian communities was one opportunity she saw as an inspired possibility for religious work. Creating a community of religious women who could move freely about in society, take professional roles and develop their careers, maintaining a deep commitment to their religious lives was an imaginative response to that possibility. While the SOS way of life was a departure from the protected and highly structured life of the religious women of Catherine's day, her vision for the Institute was not a rupture with tradition, but was a retrieval of an earlier vision of Christian community – one in which Christian leaders lived as missionary travellers, dedicated to being with those who most needed to encounter God's transforming power. Catherine embraced adventure, often speaking of the missionary life as romantic and daring.

About the mission of the SOS, she wrote,

> It is extremely religiously romantic and the definite future of our Order consists of this kind of rare challenge and conquest. All life must be supported by the soil … The future depends on what we can do for rural children and families. It is simple but not understood or acted upon by very many.

Her concern was to focus the Church's attention on the threat posed to Canadians if the culture of the family farm could not be sustained. She described this form of social activism as romantic and adventurous, because it was a resistance to more dominant trends of technology and urbanization in mainstream society.

For her, the human quest was ultimately a religious journey initiated and guided by God. Her curiosity and concern for others energized her to cross into new territories, meet new people and discover new and challenging situations. Such spirit required her to trust God to provide for her needs. The figure of Abraham, therefore – a simple human being chosen by God for a divine adventure – appealed greatly to her imagination.

Abraham, in response to God's command, set out towards a land that would be shown to him by the mysterious divine presence he had encountered. Catherine, too, set out to the West, seeing it as a land ripe with promise and opportunity. Like the proverbial Promised Land, the rich, fertile soil of the Canadian prairies offered settlers a new beginning of promise and blessing. For Abraham and his people, the journey was fraught with many temptations and dangers, yet they were called to be a distinct people in the world; they had to resist assimilation into the cultures and religious practices of other nations. As a people, they witnessed in public to God's steadfast support, while acknowledging their own failures and weaknesses. Reading the signs of the times according to this biblical theme, Catherine believed God wanted her to work among western immigrants, helping them to develop communities. New Canadian Catholics, by remembering and sharing their unique faith identity, would receive God's blessing and be a blessing to others.

As Catherine noticed, the people were without spiritual guidance. In many cases they found it difficult or impossible to sustain any kind of religious life. With little support from the established Church in Canada, some Catholic immigrants were becoming indifferent to religion, while others were joining Protestant denominations. This leakage of Catholics from the Church, as it was called, greatly concerned Catherine. Her approach focused on building Catholics' confidence so that their inherited faith tradition would be an ongoing strength to them, noting their concerns were immediately focused on everyday survival as they strove for economic and social stability. These practical needs, which were certainly real, took precedence over matters of faith in some of the homes and communities of the settlers. Spiritual guidance could help them to make their inherited faith relevant in light of their present hopes and concerns.

Catherine was moved by the settlers' need to know God's blessing in their own experience, and she was concerned about the real dangers facing them. Renewed faith would place their struggle for material gain and personal security in a new perspective. It would help to relieve some of their fears about survival in a strange and often hostile territory. In everyday encounters with the Sisters, they could be guided towards renewed faith in God's care and concern for all people. Catherine believed the settlers also needed to shoulder the religious and social responsibilities that grew from this relationship with God and neighbour. Underlying her insistence on cooperation and friendship among the new inhabitants of the West was the conviction that God's blessing was extended to *all* people through Abraham. The Catholic Church, therefore, existed for the world and its people. Education and faith development went hand in hand, Catherine argued. For her, adequately trained teachers working in rural public schools had the greatest potential for the development of Christianity and Canadian citizenship in a pluralistic population.

As mentioned earlier, Catherine's concern for Catholics' responsibility to participate in the building of society is striking since it coincided with the Church's contemporary teaching on just social development. As she reflected on, and prayed about, her experience with settlers, her life turned in a new direction, and a new phase of her spiritual journey began. In many ways this journey meant leaving behind the life she had known. As a Sister and a teacher, she would cross conventional boundaries without any certainty about how things would work out. She knew she would need faith like Abraham's if she was to be able to trust in the goodness of what lay ahead. Encouraging another Sister, she wrote, "God's real world is still good and safe. Those who have faith like Abraham's Faith (and we need it) can calmly look on – and have still stronger Faith! God will provide!" Catherine's goal was that she and her Sisters be models of Christian faith, inspiring the settlers to trust in God's provision. Trusting God, and being good neighbours in this new land, required willingness to let God lead them all into unity and solidarity, confidently expressing their faith and responsibly living with their neighbours.

Catherine's own love of the farm life and her sense of its importance for society ignited her desire to live among rural immigrants. She found farming to be noble work, a work of "basic industry" that fed the world. Via missionaries, the Church could foster a sense of religious and moral responsibility among the farmers, arising from the dignity of participating in the growing of food for the world. She believed the rich farm land of Canada's West was not only a possession to be acquired for personal gain but a gift for all Canada and the world beyond it. The theme of God's provision and humanity's absolute dependence upon God was foundational to Catherine's spirituality: human responsibility flowed from knowledge of God as the power behind all creativity and development. Reflecting on her life in the SOS while in her nursing home in St. Catharines, Ontario, Catherine left no doubt about the Sisters' need to trust and pray for God's power to do their work. "All God's people must be treated fairly – native people and newcomers. We must dare. Nothing is impossible with God and we have to talk to Him with confidence. God likes to be asked with great Faith," she wrote.

Catherine's willingness to embark on the path of religious life was obedience to that inner voice beckoning her to go and be present where God's love was needed. She believed herself to have heard God calling her onto a certain path – a path that led to a future known only to God. Like Abraham, Catherine believed there was a higher purpose associated with this quest, one that had to do with God's will. While some missionary work was being done to address social problems in the cities, Catherine followed a call to the wilderness to assist Canadians in meeting the challenge of pioneering on the frontier. Soon after experiencing this call, she found a sympathetic listener in Archbishop Neil McNeil. Jeanne Beck writes,

> Like Catherine, Archbishop McNeil was worried about the spiritual dangers and cultural isolation facing the Central European immigrants, and did his best to find priests who spoke their language so that they would become more comfortable with Canadian ways. In the days before any government aid, he urged the Catholic Churches to provide them with language classes and emergency relief, lest they lose their faith because their Church had seemingly deserted them when they were strangers in a strange land.[10]

Catherine's desire to be among the people is clearly and often stated in her letters and memoirs. Instead of seeking communion with God through contemplative solitude or the monastic life, Catherine turned towards the world of suffering and abandoned human beings. Like her model of faith, Abraham, she was sent by God to become a stranger in a new land, an emissary of God's truth and a witness to God's power. As a stranger, Abraham's status and position were uncertain. Having the faith of Abraham, then, had social ramifications for Catherine. Such faith would make her vulnerable, needing the goodwill of others.

Once Catherine discerned that God's will was for her to travel into new mission territory, she trusted God would provide all that was needed to do the work. Trust and obedience developed together. Although she struggled with obedience to hierarchical authorities, she believed she was faithful to God's will. Obedience to God, however, carries no guarantees of safety in this world. The Bible and Christian tradition offer many stories of people who were persecuted because they claimed to have authority from God. Catherine believed divine inspiration came to people who wanted to know what God was asking of them, and she knew that acting upon divine inspiration involved risk. She was fond of mentioning Joan of Arc as someone willing to listen to God and to risk herself in service of God's Church. Catherine reflected on the origins of the SOS in light of Joan of Arc's story in a letter to Sister General Mary Reansbury in 1968:

> [The SOS] would never have existed if we had waited for some bishop or even the Pope to speak up and tell us what to do. God does not work on the human spirit that way. He speaks to the individual soul as He did to the Mother of Jesus or to Joan of Arc. Bishops may oppose the idea that God provides. As they did in France a person goes ahead with a practical conviction as God wishes her to do – and she is an 'upstart' in the eyes of Clergy or the women religious of old Orders – or she is just a show-off or a nut or a 'fool.' And she must be obstructed by the humans who are sanctimonious or cheaply proud or ambitious to have power. But they are blind to the fact that God is all-powerful, that every individual has God-given rights – that Joan of Arc was not a fool nor a witch.

Joan's story caused Catherine to ponder what it means to be free under the authority of God. "I could not give up having a mind of my own, to which I had every right," she wrote. This is not to suggest Catherine would uphold the right of the individual to act in isolation from the Church, as proven by her own efforts to persuade her community, as well as to find a place within the larger community of the Church. It is simply Catherine's way of explaining that community is not always encountered as a safe place for daring people. She believed the freedom to think for herself was the gateway to public honesty. According to Sister Lena Renaud, Catherine often quoted Shakespeare as a personal declaration and teaching to other women, suggesting, "To thine own self be true; Thou canst not then be false to any man" (Hamlet, Act I, Sc. 3, 78-82).

In speaking of the need for faith like Abraham's, or of adopting the kind of missionary life exemplified by Paul, Catherine was defending her freedom to act in accordance with God's will. At 36 years of age, she was not a young girl at the time of her vocational experience and entrance into religious life. An accomplished teacher and a faithful adult member of the Catholic Church, she had gained confidence living her faith and being responsible for herself and others. She trusted God and she trusted her ability to assess needs, to determine value, and to decide upon an appropriate course of action in a given situation.

Catherine believed the responsibilities asked of people could only be truly known by people living in those particular places and times. Individuals had rights, but only insofar as those rights were used responsibly in moral living and with respect for God's authority. As she observed in stories about Abraham and in Paul's accounts, inspiration and action went together. But, as Catherine discovered, existing religious communities could not necessarily respond immediately to new insights about the needs of the Church. The path illuminated in Catherine's mind could only be followed by someone willing to step into new territory, as Father Coughlan eventually pointed out. Beck speaks about the ground-breaking nature of Catherine's proposal for religious life:

> In practice, her project meant that sisters of her new order were not to be separated from the secular world by regulations which restricted their social and religious contacts with any of the laity, Protestant or Catholic. Given the wide gulf which then existed between the Catholic and non-Catholic world, and between the lay and clerical world within Catholic society, this in itself was a revolutionary idea.[11]

In her early attempts to join a religious community, Catherine found herself confronting the institutionally mediated authority of the traditional women's religious orders. She believed the fixation on monastic order and the requirement of unquestioned obedience to superiors would only hamper achieving her unique call to live among the abandoned poor of the West. Although initially devastated by her failure to find a place within their religious community, Catherine later expressed her gratefulness for the wise discernment of the Sisters of St. Joseph, as these Sisters realized Catherine's path was leading somewhere new. Sister Avila, CSJ, had been Catherine's novice mistress during her time with the Sisters of St. Joseph in Toronto. In 1924, Sr. Avila wrote to express her happiness and excitement about Catherine's work. She advised her to place her confidence in God, saying, "God wants us to realize how all must rest on Him – our weakness the condition of His strength within – virtue thus made perfect in infirmity." Catherine faithfully followed this advice, trusting that God would supply whatever was necessary for her to respond to her religious vocation.

As we have seen, Catherine was fond of exclaiming, "God will provide!" Throughout her life, she learned to trust deeply in God's promise, surrendering herself to the divine mystery of God's will for her. Learning to surrender to God's authority was the great challenge for Abraham as he came to understand that God's plan required his total obedience. He made numerous mistakes before finally agreeing to trust God, and was even asked to sacrifice his son's future to God as a demonstration of his trust. Symbolically, this can be understood as a commitment to trust God, not only in present circumstances but also in the plans we have for our future. It was this trust that Catherine intended when she spoke of Abraham's faith. As she explained, "The Spirit of daring and of trusting in Divine help must be there. Hopes can be knocked 'hopeless' at times but 'Carry-on', says the spirit of adventure which the 'Witness of God' must possess."

While Catherine had great faith in God's plans for her, surrendering the future of the Institute she had helped to create was a lifelong struggle. Abraham's story reminded her that steadfast obedience to God could only come through trust in God's eternal faithfulness. Religious obedience was, first of all, obedience to personal conscience and responsibility. Since God's will is known in the soul of the individual, people must be free to respond to the realities of the times while remaining humble enough to do what is possible, leaving the rest to God.

Catherine's attitudes towards obedience compelled her to question the validity of a life of enclosure for Catholic women religious.

Expecting the vows of religious life to have practical consequences in the lives of the members of the Institute and in the broader community, she wrote to two Sisters,

> You each have a vast field of opportunity to be downright practical. Your patience and endurance will be greatly tested but I feel certain you can solve every problem – help all the types of human-beings with whom you have contact. Put not your trust in man. Only God is perfect!

Divine authority, Catherine argued, rests primarily with God. While she did not deny the legitimate authority of community leaders, she did acknowledge the limits of all human authority. Humans have a responsibility to question and to avoid blindly following illogical rules and customs. She proposed that God's authority was sometimes expressed as prophetic calls to the Church's leaders through the inspired vision of particular people. However, she also expressed her dismay that her obedience to God in following the *original* inspiration of the Sisters of Service sometimes appeared to be of little consequence to those who held authority in the community. "God will do as He wishes Himself. He gave us a mandate here to be attended to – not to be flung aside on account of somebody's whims. The image of our purpose as SOS has already been made too foggy."

Catherine's initial contact with the Sisters of St. Joseph in 1920 convinced her that if a new ministry was required, a new Institute should be established to work in cooperation with all of the other institutes of the Church. Before experiencing life in a religious community as a postulant with the Sisters of St. Joseph of Toronto, Catherine knew very little about life in a women's religious order. There is little doubt that there were some positive aspects of religious life that appealed to her, since she retained her respect and admiration for many Sisters from a variety of communities throughout her life. She seems to have gleaned from her experience that life in a religious community is ideally a gift of solidarity and support for the purpose of living out a common mission.

Catherine's brief experience in the St. Joseph's community, however, taught her that some of the traditional aspects of religious life, such as cumbersome apparel, long lists of rules and regulations and severe restrictions on socialization would not work in the missions she had in mind for the western rural outposts. Thirty-six years old, and a professional teacher for eighteen years, Catherine had become an independent thinker and a prudent decision maker. It was difficult to surrender to strict rules of obedience in the convent, especially those that seemed out of step with the times and denied women the right to think for themselves. During her time as a postulant, Catherine also had a hard time keeping her thoughts to herself when speaking with others. Her statements communicated her strong determination to do mission work in western Canada. Religious life in a traditional order offered Catherine no autonomy to decide for herself where she would work or what type of work she would do. She reported being told, "You will just go where you are sent." When she had entered the community, she had been under the impression that the Sisters were planning a mission in Vancouver, where she had hoped to go. Over time it became clear to her that no such plan would be realized.

Speaking of the experience with Father Coughlan in 1920, his comments to her revealed his understanding of the challenge she faced in religious life, as well as offering a way forward for Catherine. Laughing heartily, he pronounced that Catherine had likely "talked too much about the West" during her time with the Sisters of St. Joseph. His next comment spoke of the conclusion he had reached about Catherine's vision and the possibilities for religious women in her time, when he said to her, "You had better start a community of your own."

Proof of the new Institute's authentic charism would come as God provided candidates for the new mission. "God will provide suitable vocations," she wrote confidently. "This is His task. He can do it in ways no SOS could possibly think of and He cannot be pushed aside by any of His creatures." Father Coughlan believed Catherine's inspiration was genuine. He realized its powerful influence on her was part of the reason she had been unable to surrender her will in the strict way demanded by the Holy Rule of the Sisters of St. Joseph. Her call to be in the midst of those who were suffering, and her grasp of the possibility of assistance for them, was clear to her. This vision laid a claim on Catherine that never loosened its hold. Her willing obedience was directed primarily to the One she considered to be the communicator of that inspiration – her *Creator*. She believed God communicated not only *through* the Church but also *to* the Church. She submitted her will obediently to the authorities of the Church and of her Institute, although often with great resistance. Throughout her life, she remained convinced that God's power worked in the heart, mind and spirit of individuals, calling people to the holiness of love, responsibility and social justice.

When Catherine spoke about the faith of Abraham, she meant the kind of faith that sets us free to do God's will; it is ironic, therefore, that she found the hierarchical structure of the Church could mediate authority in ways that made such freedom to act difficult. Her vision for responsible ministry in rural societies, therefore, implied certain changes would be necessary in the governance of the SOS. Women in the more traditional communities were governed by the instituted rules, norms and conventions particular to their orders. All women in these orders were required to offer full obedience to their superiors, seeking special permission for everything not covered by the institutional regulations, even in the most trivial affairs of their lives.

The active lives of SOS missionary workers, especially those involved in professions like teaching and nursing, made it necessary for individuals to be able to judge and decide for themselves in a range of situations. While the ideal was still to respect those placed in positions of authority in the community, Catherine knew local superiors would need to respect the intelligence and moral integrity of the Sisters in the field if the missions were to run effectively. She explained to Sister Madge Barton, an adventurous teaching Sister whom Catherine greatly respected, that the SOS "must have a clear understanding that we know ourselves how much we can do, and what we do in our church work, etc., must be left to our own volition." The absence of clergy in many of the rural settlements added a further dimension to the innovations of the SOS missions, since the Sisters were expected to live out their responsibilities without the direct supervision of local priests. Catherine frequently mentioned conflict with pastors in rural communities. In a May 1968 letter to Sister Barton she wrote, "Pastors can be the worst slave drivers ever." It is clear that she did not let unfortunate encounters with certain priests define her relationship with clergy, however, since she counted many priests among her good friends, trustworthy guides and spiritual advisors. Her conflicts with priests arose from their expectations concerning the Sisters' activities. The priests who particularly drew Catherine's ire were those who either did not understand or who refused to respect the Sisters' particular mandate and their authority to act.

Catherine sensed that many of the practices of religious communities revealed the Church's nostalgia for the world of medieval custom. One element of setting out in her new religious life meant leaving these outdated practices behind. She repeatedly warned the Sisters of Service against "falling into old grooves," which was her way of voicing her prophetic call to the community. She knew that moving away from this conventional form of religious life was quite radical, but the mission of the SOS depended upon the Sisters being friends with other members of society. Relationships with people outside the traditional convent were closely monitored, or even avoided altogether. She needed a new image of the active life of a religious. Abraham's life of nomadic wandering, trusting in God's providence and guidance, seems a very apt symbol for Catherine's faith in light of her vision for the Sisters in the West.

Throughout her religious life, Catherine found resonance with the spirituality of the apostle Paul – her patron Saint. She was inspired by his way of life, his manner of handling conflict among different Christian communities, and his willingness to confront social and religious problems. She formed many of her principles for ministry in the rural communities by reflecting on Paul's attitudes towards Christian community and religious reform. She also took a lesson from his courageous endurance in the religious life. As Catherine's close companion during her later years, Sister Lena Renaud, pointed out, Sister Donnelly "got to admire Paul for his dogged perseverance and deep faith in suffering and in whatever he undertook."

Paul's writings reveal what he believed to be happening in his own time. Catherine's writings are delivered in the same style. While she narrated much of what was happening in the world, she intended people to grasp the theological significance of these events. Paul's reflections drew upon the prophecy of the Hebrew Scriptures, in particular those prophecies that concerned the *coming* reign of God. Paul believed in God's promise to establish a reign of power on earth that would never be overturned. This theme of God's reign – kingdom – carries throughout the Hebrew Bible. Consider, for instance, the following prophetic utterance from the book of Daniel: "And in the days of those kings the God of Heaven will set up a kingdom that shall never be destroyed, nor shall this kingdom be left to another people" (Daniel 2:44). Paul interpreted this prophetic text for his own time, and Catherine followed his example by professing her belief that God was indeed establishing God's kingdom on earth.

There are some parallels between Catherine's insistence that the SOS must embark on a path different from that of the established religious orders and Paul's insistence that he had been given authority by God to embark on his mission to the Gentiles. Both referred to the faith of Abraham – trust in God and obedience to God's will – as a foundation for their unique spiritualities. In Paul's vision, Christian communities would inevitably be a sign of contradiction as one form of power fell and God's power took over. This theme in his writings exerted a strong influence on Catherine's spirituality. Her communication strategy, therefore, was much like Paul's: she witnessed to the qualities of genuine Christian communities by listing them as evidence that conversion to the reign of God was taking place.

Catherine's reflections led her to believe that community development took a distinct form when it grew in relationships of faith, love and cooperation – and that communities manifesting these qualities were living signs of God's reign on earth. She preferred missionary work that remained close to these practical developmental roots. The qualities that Paul listed in his letters came about through faithful living that bore fruit in religious and moral responsibility. To the Corinthians he wrote,

> We are putting no obstacle in anyone's way, so that no fault may be found with our ministry, but as servants of God we have commended ourselves … through great endurance, in afflictions, hardships, calamities, beatings, imprisonments, riots, labours, sleepless nights, hunger, by purity, knowledge, patience, kindness, holiness of spirit, genuine love, truthful speech, and the power of God. (2 Corinthians 6:3-7)

The influence of Paul's advice surfaces in one of Catherine's letters to Sister Madge Barton in 1966:

> You know it is the kindness of the sisters, their generosity and resourcefulness with poor or afflicted people, their interest in every child, that have really influenced the people and drawn them towards the Church. It is more the example of the teachers' lives day by day that has done the trick – more than a period of religion teaching in school.

Catherine advocated a simple and inconspicuous entrance into rural communities. Sisters were witnesses to God's love, people who invited imitation. She identified those characteristics of the prevailing culture that were obstacles to Christian community development. Living lives of holiness as signs of God's power within the dominant culture, the Sisters were to encourage others to do the same. To add another dimension to their work, she also proposed they stand as a challenge *within* the Church, wearing contemporary clothes and adapting their Rule for practical reasons related to the needs of all. Her remarkable flexibility regarding institutional practices demonstrated her understanding that the institutions of people, under the influence of the Holy Spirit, must be constantly transformed and renewed.

Paul witnessed to the Christian community how the institutions of this world that were symbols of domination and oppression were being transformed as the reign of God manifested in history. He expected Christians to develop all of the characteristics of this reign so they could take part in this great transformation. Like Paul, Catherine intended a very practical outcome in her ministry: the dynamic of the Holy Spirit coming to life in human community.

Catherine envisioned, for example, that financial aid from local governments would flow to the SOS to support their missionary work. She reasoned that, like Paul and his companions, Sisters would find a place among the people as valuable community members considered worthy of their wages. In her memoir, she wrote, "The funds earned by teaching and paid by the government of the province would make me and others independent of any extensive help from anyone. In this line, St. Paul's principles were mine." She believed that eventually the Institute could be a self-supporting ministry of the Church if its professional women earned their wages from the people they served. She knew this to be a radical innovation in the support of women's religious activities but, as she explained in one of her histories of the community,

> I had attended a public school as a child, had never been taught by nuns, nor even by Catholic lay teachers. I had learned how to get along with people of all faiths and yet be strong in my own. The rural public schools of the West could afford a livelihood (St. Paul's style). We could contact Catholic children and homes in this way. The new community was to work where other orders had not ventured.

As Catherine interpreted Paul, missionary work must become an integrated and valued form of work within developing communities – not an alien form of activity entering the community. This meant becoming a contributing and valued member of the society in which she lived. This understanding was to have a radical influence on her attitudes towards women's resourcefulness in ministry, marrying in her mind the two streams of religious formation and professional development.

Catherine was confident of the value of the conjoined religious and professional work she would be doing in the rural areas. She believed the work of the SOS to be of *universal* value for all citizens and therefore worthy of a fair wage. If Catholics intended to support missions financially by seeking donations from other, better established parts of the country, she feared people would be suspicious of the motives of the missionaries, especially because questions of language rights and religious denominational rights had created tensions. As she understood Paul, he claimed workers for the Church were worthy of being supported by communities, however poor. Supporting their own faith development, if initiated at early stages in the life of the community, would soon be understood as a responsibility in the lives of community members. SOS could be professionally employed by becoming legitimately qualified in teaching or nursing, abiding by provincial law and government regulations. This would cultivate trust and respect for the work of the Sisters, whose work would be sustained because of its social value. Catherine knew Paul encountered obstacles in advancing his principles for the growth of Christian communities. She was keenly aware of the differences in their situations, but she highlighted some qualities in Paul's spirituality to validate her approach to community development and Catholic social responsibility. Like Paul, she remained committed and consistent in communicating the inspiration behind her vision. Each shared a sense of urgency in following well-defined paths of vocation. Each felt the pressures of time, meaning there was work to be done in the building up of Christian communities.

Like Paul, Catherine urged cooperation and endurance in the face of grave obstacles. His accounts also influenced her economic and social vision. Paul entered into communities, listening to learn what their unique problems were and helping community members to come up with solutions in light of their Christian faith. He availed himself of the generosity of people because he was not afraid to demonstrate his need for them. All were equals in God's reign – people with diverse gifts who shared in the unity of the Body of Christ. With his help they learned that acts of generosity, compassion, gratefulness and forgiveness were outward signs of a spiritual practice of Christian faith. Life in the Holy Spirit resisted the human tendency towards systems of domination and entitlement that divided human societies or created systems of privilege.

Catherine believed in these principles of development. Faith that God was at work in subtle, hidden ways convinced her that the trials of life were purposeful. She admired Paul's insistence that the reign of God was possible among all people, and that it had radical implications for the social and economic life of every community where Christians actively lived out their baptismal call. That call to public expression of faith appealed to her. Paul's experience of conversion caused him to seek a new way of living out his traditional Jewish faith in public, as expressed in Richard Horsley and Neil Silberman's work, *The Message and the Kingdom: How Jesus and Paul Ignited a Revolution and Transformed the Ancient World*:

> Instead of continuing to serve the established institutions of the Jewish community in Damascus and the Temple Hierarchy in Jerusalem – and thereby passively accepting the rule of Rome as the will of God and a fact of nature – he looked forward to a new era of human existence, in which life on earth would be transformed.[12]

Catherine was inspired by Paul's commitment to Christian leadership as a form of self-sacrificing service. Serving God meant helping people take part in the transformation of the world begun in Christ. The Gospel broke down all the old barriers to unity among those seeking a shared future under the reign of God. She was attracted to Paul's dynamic sense of outward mission – his *active* and public religious life. This action involved taking the message on the road, entering new public spaces with the intention of encouraging the transformation of society for the good of all.

A concern for the early development of Christian communities drew Catherine to notice Paul's missionary strategies and reinforced her understanding of faith as the kind of trust modelled by Abraham. As a missionary of extraordinary skill, Paul drew upon the faith of Abraham as inspiration for his courageous and daring ministry of serving Christ in the world. Catherine referred to Paul often as she described the course and development of her own ministry work among rural frontier inhabitants. These two figures – Abraham and Paul – influenced the development of her spirituality by offering her models of self-surrender, ingenuity, courage and endurance.

❧ Chapter Five ❧

A Spirituality of Ministry, Mission and Adventure

What has been done is only a forerunner of what is possible
by experimenting perseveringly.

Let nothing discourage you!

Sister Catherine Donnelly, in a letter to Bishop Routhier

Catherine consistently demonstrated great passion for her teaching ministry and missionary work. She was a woman of considerable physical stamina whose daring spirit, sense of humour and optimism helped her to endure the harsh conditions of the Canadian West. In 1924, following Novitiate and first profession of vows, she headed west to Camp Morton, Manitoba, determined "to convince others that a new field of labor was open for inspired workers." In the early days of the Sisters of Service (SOS), the Sisters were still actively discerning their new place in society. In each place they set up missions, they became fully integrated members of the broader community. In this new style of religious life in the Church, women took on roles and responsibilities that had not been part of traditional religious life for Roman Catholic nuns.

Catherine and other Sisters of Service worked doggedly, setting up teaching and health care missions in small rural communities on the prairies. It was exhausting work, but Catherine was determined to do all she could to nurture these rural missions, hoping to prove the feasibility of her plans. As she pointed out, "It would be pioneering in an entirely practical way. Conviction would come to others through factual proof, and not through any mere theory of mine." Things did not always go smoothly in these rural missions. Catherine was as conscientious about standing firm against misuse of Sisters' energies and injustice, and against intolerance in the communities as she was about working cooperatively with people. At Camp Morton, for example, Catherine ran into problems with the board of trustees, who had been using the schoolhouse for dances, after which the teachers were expected to clean up the mess. Catherine informed them that this was against provincial regulations and, when things did not improve, she contacted the Department of Education.

More than once, Catherine's insistence on proper boundaries and respect between the Sisters and other community leaders led to serious conflicts. She frequently mentioned her anger at the attitudes of some clergy members who treated women as inferior to males or saw them as fit only for more domestic tasks in the Church. The Sisters were living quite responsibly and tending to their own affairs and she believed they should be treated as professionals and equals in the mission field as well as in the Church. Those Sisters who taught in public schools were employees of the provincial government as well as members of a religious Institute. They required trustees and community members to provide the most basic necessities, such as resources for their housing and for schools as part of their teaching contracts. In a few missions, like the one at Sinnett, Saskatchewan, Catherine was dismayed by the lack of support offered to the Sisters by the parish priest, trustees and the people of the town.

These clashes, although infrequent, seem understandable. The traditional women's religious orders required the presence of a convent before the Sisters would be sent into a community. The Sisters of Service set up and managed their own houses and had a host of other duties as well, including teaching and nursing duties, pastoral visiting, and religious instruction of Catholic children. They could also be expected to lead small Catholic congregations in saying the rosary, singing, and reading the Gospel on Sundays when there was no priest to preside at the liturgy. Their early Rule described the SOS as auxiliaries to the priests, a new role that sometimes clashed with earlier views of the relationship between clergy and women religious.

Soon after Catherine envisioned the path she desired to follow in serving the people of the West, she understood the need for a reformed model of religious life for women. She bravely offered herself as a radical experiment in missionary life. Father Coughlan, as spiritual advisor to the Sisters, prepared them for the experience of letting go of everything to follow God's call. All adventure requires a willingness to accept risks, and the Sisters often experienced these risks as personal sacrifices freeing them for service. Even as Catherine grew older and unable to venture out into the mission field, she coaxed the Sisters, "Now is the time for you young Sisters to dare fearlessly with all your might and trust in God." She considered the sacrifices of religious life a gateway into the joyful adventure of discovering and cooperating with the will of God.

After Catherine experienced the adventure of missionary treks in British Columbia, her focus in ministry and missionary work became more fixed on the dynamic of personal encounter. While the teaching of doctrine and religious tradition were always important to her, her letters began to stress the practical influence of the Sisters in the dynamic of community building. They also reveal that she studied Father A.L. McIntyre and learned from his way with the settlers – an insight she attempted to carry into her own ministry. Already in her 50s, she and Sister Irene Faye, a 24-year-old novice from Toronto, ventured into the wilds of the Cariboo Mountains by car. Often camping in forests amidst giant trees by the beautiful Fraser and Thompson rivers, they visited the remote farms of isolated settlers and gathered the children for religious instruction. Catherine revelled in the challenge of this missionary work and expressed her joy at the opportunity to reach these abandoned people. She recorded her adventures in letters and journals of this time:

> We reached the Pea Vine Valley, south of the Fraser River Banks, where live the family farthest away. We brought out two girls who are to be instructed for First Holy Communion. They will stay with people nearer here. On the way back, we called for children until the car overflowed, brought a load to the school and returned for another, taught for two hours and drove two loads part of the way home again, then came to our camp in the woods here for our supper. It was 7 P.M. We had not had a spare moment to have lunch since 10 in the morning. The road to Pea Vine is the usual type you find anywhere beside the Fraser River, dropping and climbing by switch-back trails, narrow stretches of road cut from the rock high on the edge of the precipice, slow and careful driving ....

Catherine was drawn to this pioneering style of missionary work. She relished crossing geographical, linguistic, religious, social and cultural boundaries to reach those she hoped to serve. In the process, her spirituality was increasingly expressed through innovative and socially oriented ministry. This way of life would become widespread among communities of women religious after Vatican II's reforms in the 1960s, but in Catherine's time it was unheard of in Canada. In these early years, Catherine interpreted the Gospel message as one calling her to social action among neglected people.

Father McIntyre proved to be a vital resource, demonstrating the qualities of the ideal missionary in his endless enthusiasm, his easy way with all types of people and his ecumenical orientation. Most of all, Catherine admired his deep love of the settlers and his desire to respond to their spiritual needs. Sharing in their poverty, and in their isolation from the more populated centres, Father McIntyre came to live among the poor humbly and with deep compassion. This seems to have forever etched the image of the journeying missionary in Catherine's mind. These experiences of missionary work affirmed for her that what she wanted was to take up this adventurous lifestyle, following Christ in brave and self-sacrificing ways.

During these early years of the SOS, Catherine began to learn and practise a form of missionary work that focused on grassroots development of Christian community. In the Cariboo, she experienced the spiritual dynamics of personal relationships between missionaries and settlers. She realized that the conditions and realities of life in the missions must influence the Church's understanding of the settlers' spiritual needs and allow for freedom in ministry.

The settlers she encountered faced challenges such as loneliness, alienation, low self-esteem, ignorance and poverty, so they welcomed and appreciated the personal concern of the missionaries, the Sisters' guiding influence with the children, and the promise of further connection with the Church. During these trips, Catherine began to truly understand the spiritual value of the Sisters' contact with the settlers. The homesteaders responded to the missionaries with their own generosity, hard work and friendship. In 1936, she wrote home regarding people's shyness towards the Sisters: "Naturally the people are a bit shy at first about having the Sisters come into their houses." At first, she recommended having the Sisters bring everything they needed with them, since they "aren't offered food and have to ask for it." Soon, however, she began recounting the generosity of the settlers who were supplying food, fixing up their campsite lodgings, and helping them when they got stuck on the road. During her 1936 trip, she made the following observation: "The calling on the people and the listening to their accounts of trials and struggles and helping them where possible with what information or friendly advice we can give seems almost as important and effective as the teaching of the children." Catherine grew to understand the empowering force of true missionary work, as the people helped the Sisters to help them. For her, this mutual responsibility was a simple beginning for genuine Christian community. Her reflections on these encounters deepened her awareness of the importance of community life in the life of the Church.

Catherine's accounts of the Cariboo trips show how her grasp of the real value of the missionary treks grew over time. Her first reports focused on the practical difficulties faced by the Sisters, mentioning harrowing travel conditions, and the hard work of finding and gathering the children for religious instruction and sacramental preparation. She observed and analyzed the conditions: crudeness among the children and adults, lack of education, little health care, poor hygiene, no Church presence, dire poverty, unmarried couples and unbaptized children.

In later reports, however, analytical observations transformed into animated accounts of meetings with the settlers, detailing how the Sisters' presence and teaching evoked the settlers' interest in their Catholic faith. They spoke of the people's gestures of generosity, welcome and friendship towards the SOS. Catherine came to believe that the Sisters' teaching of Catholic doctrine was best expressed in subtle ways, through these personal encounters. The Sisters' lived expression of the truths of Catholic doctrine inspired the community's growth in generosity, welcome and friendship. She began to understand that the Sisters' primary focus must be on Christian encounter. Friendship, growth in charity and trust and interest in the Church were, for her, genuine signs of the reality of God's kingdom and of the success of the SOS's missions. She believed these would become the raw materials for the growth of Christian communities in the West.

Contemporary reflection reveals the importance of the *theology* of the Church's missionaries – that is, a person's knowledge of God and of what God desires from humans, who are made in God's image. In Christian theology, knowledge of God has a great deal to do with understanding what it means to be human. When Catherine considered people's growth in holiness, she reflected on the individual's intimate relationship with God, as well as on the practical social implications of personal holiness. This approach to spiritual development echoes the words recorded in the Book of Micah, which Catherine underlined in her Bible: "He has told you, O mortal, what is good; and what does the Lord require of you but to do justice, and to love kindness and to walk humbly with your God?" (Micah 6:8).

Believing in the sacredness of all life, Catherine knew knowledge of God is wisdom with practical value in the human world. She often noted that the Holy Spirit was at work in all true Christians, so there was no reason not to cooperate with one another. The Holy Spirit's activity, wherever encountered, was an invitation to seek to know the Spirit at work both in the Church and in the broader society. This was different from the model of Catholic faith focusing on private holiness and perfection, which often led to "disdain for the world." Catherine knew withdrawing from the world behind the convent walls meant women would not be able to venture into areas where needy people awaited the Church's workers.

Catherine was attuned to the harmony and unity operating in the world. Influenced by her Celtic heritage, she believed the earth to be a good place to learn about God's promise, protection and concern for human beings. She was thus interested in helping others identify and respond to the opportunities made possible by the grace of God. Her spirituality of ministry and mission focused on the practical reality of God's love and its implications for human life. The theology that supported Catherine's ministry was influenced by her integrated view of the world of matter and spirit. Irish theologian Diarmuid O'Murchú has called attention to some of the features of an integrated spirituality; most of these qualities are exhibited in Catherine's stated beliefs and in her actions. She focused on complementing existing institutions with something new. She resisted simplifying the situation of the Church in the world but tried to act in ways benefiting everyone, rather than choosing one group over all others. She strove for what was good without denying the real problem of evil and avoided simple blame by trying to understand the underlying causes of people's problems. She knew processes take time – and sometimes a long time – to unfold in the way God intends. She believed that, in a world of diversity, people of different backgrounds and beliefs can share in leadership.[13]

Catherine's experience of mysticism was, at heart, profoundly practical, and her very existence was an encounter into which she could gaze for signs of God's life. God does not call us out of the world to a distant place, but calls the baptized quite decidedly into the world to participate in the mission of Christ. Jesus is *Emmanuel*, meaning "God with us." Catherine took this real presence of God as the basis for her ministry. Jesus' revelation of God's active presence in the world had practical implications for how Christians should be disposed towards

God and one another. Imitation of her divine model was imitation of God's outreach to all human beings. This imitation was based on the revelation of God's solidarity with human beings, and God's compassion, which we have encountered in Jesus.

In the religious life of the Sisters of Service who were so involved in their broader communities, it was a challenge to balance the active life with daily prayer and devotions. Many Redemptorist practices were part of the SOS spirituality, such as visits to the Blessed Sacrament and saying the rosary. It was also necessary to find time for quiet prayer in the midst of such a busy life. It is not surprising, therefore, that Catherine insisted that a chapel be part of every Sisters of Service home. Writing to Sister Patricia Burke about this matter, she said, "A Catholic Christian believes in very earnest and undisturbed prayer. Besides, having a chapel in our house is an example to all people – an indication that God takes first place in our lives." Catherine seems to have considered prayer an ongoing conversation with her Creator, an activity that meshed seamlessly with day-to-day activities and practical responsibilities. This is illustrated in a somewhat humorous way in a letter written by Sister Mary Quinn, SOS, the Superior of the hospital mission at Edson, to Sister General Margaret Guest at the Motherhouse in Toronto. While Catherine was spending some time recuperating at St. John's Hospital in Edson in 1940, Sister Quinn objected to Catherine "bringing her mending to chapel and draping it over the organ."

Both Catherine's active intellect and busy lifestyle were a challenge in her prayer life, and in later years she intimated that she wished she had taken more time for prayer. By this, she likely meant the type of prayer that calls a person to silence, reverence and contemplation. Those who knew her best witnessed her constant reading of Scriptures and the way she related biblical and current events as a way of reflecting on God's will. By nature a very active and talkative woman, she could be awed and silenced by the beauty of creation. She loved to walk in the forest at Camp Morton, near the shores of Lake Winnipeg, prayerfully contemplating the wonders of nature. In her later years, Catherine's prayer life became a central concern for her, especially after she became unable to read. During the last years of her life, she took to wearing her rosary around her neck so it would be close at hand. In fact, Sister Lena Renaud said that, at times, Sister Donnelly prayed so hard that it was necessary to repair the links of her rosary beads!

With such a practical approach to religious life, Catherine's vocation led her into a world of novelty, challenge and opportunity. She related,

> Until I came over the Rockies from Alberta into the precipitous and secluded trails of the Cariboo I had no idea that such conditions existed so near to me. Now, to my mind, Alberta is 'way back east,' in the size of her parishes, and the frequenting of the church buildings. Even the Peace River District could hardly compare as a field of missionary adventure to that of the wild Fraser.

Catherine found adventure in ministry spiritually transforming, and she brought to life through her actions what she learned. The daring, bravery and courage of SOS women became, for her, the romance of the missionary quest. She imagined the SOS leading the whole Church towards fulfilment of its mission to foster and promote practical Christian unity. To risk bravely, abandoning herself to the glorious cause of missionary work, was a way of radically placing her trust in God. This trust bore fruit in bringing the presence of the Church to those who would not otherwise encounter it. As she wrote, "We just must continue frontier work – pioneering where other Sisterhoods cannot operate like we do. This would give our Sisters a worthwhile challenge – adventure – religious romance. 'Launch out into the Deep' is easy to say and sounds brave – but we really must do it." Catherine found daring and desire for adventure essential qualities of her missionary life. They were necessary to propel her across conventional boundaries towards a more vivid and inspiring encounter with God and neighbour.

Catherine's theology of mission as encounter was practical, but it was anything but dull. She intended the spirituality of the SOS to be characterized by courage and bravery. Her mind was set on religious life as a quest – not for personal fulfilment alone, but for fulfilment of the divine mission on earth. The nature of the search was to resist the temptation of comfortable conventions in religious life and to grow in trust and faith by letting God lead the way. Writing to Sister Madge Barton, Catherine stressed the developmental nature of mission, urging, "…we are to be in our territory and not in old grooves – or fields of older communities … We must constantly practice and improve our technique."

Due to her strong sense of God's presence in the world, coupled with her drive for Catholic social action, Catherine was uneasy about any work that distanced the Sisters from the needy settlers. She understood her place to be working alongside them. And she expressed it: "'Go and teach all nations' does not mean [living] in a city house and teach them by 'remote control.'" Therefore, for example, the Sisters who worked in the religious correspondence schools in Edmonton and Regina used the postal service to correspond with families in remote locations, but during the summer catechetical tours, they met many of their correspondence students and their families. Although the work of the correspondence schools was an alternative to the original mission plan – and Catherine admittedly found the office work boring – it did offer the possibility of journeying in the mission territory. After these experiences, Catherine advocated more insistently that daring and courageous adventure were part and parcel of the true missionary life. As she said, "It is fine to pray. 'More good is wrought by prayer etc' but also, I am convinced that 'More good is wrought by dare than this world dreams of.'" Her encounters with God in prayer transformed her desire for adventure into action in her world.

As the mission of the SOS expanded to include city hostels, catechetical centres, and immigration work at Canadian ports, the rural western missions assumed a place of relative importance within the overall scope of the Institute's concerns. When Catherine agitated for a return to this primary mission field, she was not only speaking about staying faithful to the original vocation of the Institute. She also desired a certain way of life for the women who entered the community – one that would introduce them to the type of adventures in ministry that gave her so much spiritual joy and fulfilment. She was concerned with the Sisters' personal growth in faith and vitality. The SOS regarded the importance of Catherine's adventurous spirit shortly after she died. "With her passing she left us the legacy of hope for the future," read a short notice sent out by the SOS after her death. "This is our heritage. Her spirit of adventure and daring must be caught up so that we as a community may carry the torch and continue the dream she dreamed some sixty-one years ago."

If spiritual formation in the SOS included missionary adventure and the professional challenges of working in developing communities, Catherine believed the Sisters would gather memories of successful experiences of bravery and courage that would inspire and fortify them. Warning against any tendency to become comfortable in the religious life, she wrote, "Many conditions … today can discourage Sisters and cause them to look for protection for themselves – new ministries to keep them busy. SOS must be daring and step forward – not backward into what has for centuries been work older Orders could do."

Catherine's own adventurous spirit was born of her faith in God's supporting and creative presence, always available and calling her into new life. This ministerial attitude was one of her contributions to the reform of religious life for women to be more fully articulated at the time of Vatican II. The following statement, written by Father Grant Jahnke, OMI, after Catherine's death, draws attention to her brave spirit and links it to the command of Jesus:

> Catherine Donnelly's message to her Sisters and to the Church was, 'Launch into the deep. Don't hold back because there are risks. If there is a work to be done, obstacles must be demolished. God will provide the means if we but seek them.' This was the life Catherine Donnelly lived. This is her legacy to the Church.[14]

This statement references Luke's Gospel, in which Jesus tells Simon to set off into the deep water and to put his nets out for a catch of fish. This story ends as the quintessential call to participate in Christ's mission on earth. Catherine lived for this mission, and as the years went by and her physical stamina began to decline, she often reminded others that her desire was as strong as ever. It is clear she came to miss the excitement of heading off into new and uncharted fields. At the age of 84, she wrote, "If I could only throw off 20 or 30 years I'd be off to one of these northern places where SOS teachers, and health and welfare workers are needed."

To understand Catherine's drive, and particularly her ecumenical attitude, one needs to appreciate the relationship between her theology and her view of the world. Catherine witnessed to the ultimate unity of all created life and believed God to be involved with humanity in real and concrete ways. Therefore, she developed a *practical theology*. Faced with the challenge of so many diverse forms of Christianity, Catherine looked beyond apparent divisions to the ultimate oneness of God's people. She believed all were free to be uniquely themselves; differences of doctrine need not stand in the way of recognizing essential unity. While differing in significant ways, all genuinely Christian people were part of the whole creation and under God's authority. Experience taught Catherine to believe life in the Holy Spirit frees people to accept this dynamic diversity in unity.

A common tendency among Christian theologians of Catherine's time was to gain intellectual knowledge about God and then apply it to the world. Catherine, however, considered the world to be a place where God encountered humans, inviting them to respond to their encounter with the divine. Theology meant more than simply applying what was already known – there was an element of learning involved in relating to God's creation. Intimate personal relationship with God was sought through developing the interior life of the intellect, the emotions and the spirit. This search involved a communal relationship of believers and non-believers alike. Catherine's practical theology moved her to integrate the activity of thinking about God with her experience of personal relationship with God in the world.

Since Catherine's relationship with God led her out into the world to serve others, theology was an ongoing conversation with the divine in the midst of everyday life. She allowed God's real and present power to influence and guide her activity. Her practical theology motivated her to propose an active and adventurous form of religious life. At the root of her motivations were three strong convictions: that God would provide all that was needed for the mission, that God had set before her a path that she must follow, and that she had made a fundamental decision to obey God. Catherine's certainty about the truth of these convictions was not expressed in the form of a theory. It was expressed in her willingness to *set out* on the mission and to endure until she had faithfully lived out the task God had given her.

Catherine's ecumenical outlook was a simple but elegant grasp of the unity of all things in God's creation, a practical theology that is "more 'verb-like' than 'noun-like,' and … could also be called 'practicing theology.'"[15] Catherine's model grew out of her belief that God, and God alone, was the ground of all unity. Although humans are free to disregard God's call to unity, no human action could ultimately alter that reality. This vision of reality, and her focus on God's activity in the world, shaped her understanding of the need to reach out to others spiritually, finding common spiritual ground. This understanding gave her vision its inner consistency and guided her into the daring and adventurous activities of frontier missionary work: "Ecumenism was and is a most beautiful thing," she wrote. "It is growing at ground level …." Unity was the essential framework of God's creation for Catherine, understood as a basic operating principle. Catherine's theology, therefore, influenced her ministry in practical ways.

At the time of Vatican II, the Roman Catholic Church expressed its desire to "cooperate actively and positively with our separated sisters and brothers, who profess the charity of the gospel along with us, and also with all who long for true peace" (*Gaudium et spes*). The council accepted that the ecumenical movement was "a sign of the Holy Spirit's action and said that it considered the promotion of this movement to be one of its principle tasks."[16] A new spirit of dialogue and cooperation was anticipated. The council's expression stemmed from its recognition that, in spite of differences, the work of the Holy Spirit is visible in the development of Christianity outside of the Catholic Church.

One aspect of the shift at Vatican II was a new openness on the part of the Church to cooperate with other Christians to promote the Gospel. This implied a new direction which would avoid the previous tendency to seek unity among the Christian churches by re-establishing the authority of the Catholic Church, and by insisting on total agreement on questions of doctrine. A new spirit of cooperation was anticipated, reflecting the desire for unity and exhibiting respect for difference among Christian denominations. Long before the council, however, even Catherine's earliest expressions of ecumenism resonated strongly with the spirit of the ecumenical movement. She believed Father Coughlan shared her spirit and was therefore able to understand the wisdom behind her plans for the West. For her, ecumenism was a growing knowledge of the unity among Christians; human beings were becoming aware of ecumenical possibilities because of the revelation of the Holy Spirit. The ecumenical process was unfolding within creation as part of the creative activity of God. The title of her work, *Ecumenism Blossoms*, reflects her understanding of ecumenism in terms of an organic reality, that Christian unity can be attributed to God's creative processes. Catherine's efforts place her squarely in the ecumenical movement leading up to the council. Her acceptance and admiration of all Christians, her openness to their views and her willing cooperation with them in shared projects for human development are all signs of her ecumenical openness. She zealously embarked on the adventure of crossing religious boundaries to seek common ground with others whose views differed. She challenged classical religious views when based upon narrow understandings that did not grasp the possibilities of ecumenism and unity.

Catherine consistently referred to ecumenism as the unity of Christians being revealed by God in the lives of people. She required only small signs of cooperation in order to be convinced of the reality of ecumenical possibilities. Aware of the possibilities for ecumenical activity in the West, for example, she spoke of the types of cooperation that already existed there. These were, in her mind, activities to build on. While she did not deny the need or desire for discussion among experts from the various Christian denominations, she believed theoretical differences should not prevent united Christian action for justice. In a letter to Sister Patricia Burke in 1978, Catherine spoke about her experience in 1920, noting, "Ecumenism was already existing to be used." It is certain she did not mean doctrinal agreement, but rather grassroots cooperation among Christians. She found the dire needs facing communities in the rural West offered opportunities for open-minded Christian leaders to guide cooperation and development among citizens. Basic participation among the faithful, whatever their denomination, bore the qualities of Christian relationship Catherine called ecumenism.

The Catholic Church learned a great deal from Vatican II, the documents of which speak of the activity of the Holy Spirit in the Church and the world. They also address the Church's relationship with the modern world. Having witnessed the dynamic events leading up to the council, and the many reforms it ushered in, Catherine wrote "Service By Canadian Women" in 1978 as an open letter to her community. In this piece, she wrote about the relationship between the early inspiration of the SOS and this new attitude expressed in the council's teachings and example:

> To a few people it had become known that the School Laws of the western provinces would in no way prevent qualified teachers of a new Religious Order, and Health and Welfare workers from giving excellent service in many ways. Their witness in the classrooms (of God and His Laws) would be a tremendous influence on the youth of today, who are the adults of tomorrow. ... Saintly, humble, peace-loving Father Coughlan remained faithful and hopeful. His way was a ministry of love for all of God's people ... His life was one of love for all of God's people. No chauvinism, no worldly pride, no hope for worldly reward. Such a profound faith and activating love were not any too contagious, but there was already a growth in ecumenical thinking. It had started and was soon to be strengthened through the influence of Pope John XXIII and Vatican Council II. Through the fog of old customs the light of Truth was shining.

Catherine felt a resonance between the spirit of the community's founders and the spirit of Vatican II. Stories abound in the SOS community of Catherine's passion for the changes and innovations that resulted from the council. The early designs of the Institute, the beliefs and values expressed by its founders, and their theology of ministry and mission, all anticipated many of the topics that would guide the council's discussions. Innovations in the Catholic tradition had developed according to the spirituality of the founders and their cooperative action in responding to the needs of the Church and the world.

Through the lens of Vatican II, it is possible to look at Catherine's radical openness in making herself available to the Church of her day. Although she did not offer reflective commentary on the qualities of her own spirituality in her letters and writings, her comments about other people's spirituality reveal a great deal about her own spiritual values. In her acknowledgements of Father Coughlan's support throughout their long relationship, for example, she indicates that she found much in common between their spiritualities, implying that she considered the spirituality of the Redemptorists to be inspiring and supportive of her own.

Catherine chose words and terms like peace-loving, ecumenical, humble, socially aware, discerning, influential, witnessing, a ministry of love for all God's people, activating love, concern for development and reform to describe Father Coughlan's spirituality. All these qualities manifest in relationships as fruits of God's love. Catherine's spirituality resonated with this way of practising Christian faith in community and society. She chose these attributes of Father Coughlan's as ones that supported her own convictions about the public expression of faith, indicating a development that was taking place in the Church and in the world during her lifetime, as well as speaking of her desire to participate in this development.

Vatican II built upon an ongoing adjustment in the focus of the Church. The social document *Rerum Novarum*, issued in 1891, just seven years after Catherine's birth, signalled a shift in the Church's attention towards the problems of developing societies and the question of human dignity. Subsequent encyclicals supported the development of the Church's concern for social justice. By the time of the Second Vatican Council, particularly evident in the documents on The Church in the Modern World (*Gaudium et spes*) and The Dogmatic

Constitution on the Church (*Lumen gentium*), Catholics were urged to take an active part in the development of their societies on behalf of all, in light of the Gospel. When Pope John XXIII opened Vatican II in 1962, Catherine was 78. Her vibrant spirituality had been lived actively and publicly to that point, meaning that she was not only a witness to these changes, but also an active participant in bringing them about.

Catherine's vision for Catholic women religious was a foretaste of what would become a widespread transformation in the life of the Church after the council concluded in 1965. Sister Margaret Brennan, a Sister of the Immaculate Heart of Mary (IHM) and professor emerita of Regis College in Toronto, is one of many who lived through the reforms of Vatican II. She reflects in her memoirs that in the early 1950s, Pius XII recommended that women religious "update their lives in light of the changing culture."[17] After Vatican II, most communities began to heed this advice and move out of their conventional ways of life. Crossing the threshold from life in the convent to active and socially engaged ministry was an adventure that demanded a daring spirit. Sister Brennan suggests that this new adventurous spirit was, in her experience, one of the *fruits* of Vatican II. As she witnessed,

> After Vatican II, in spite of the initial reluctance of American religious congregations to follow the suggestions of Pius XII, women religious again took up the challenge, this time with greater enthusiasm. In doing so, we reflected the American tendency to embrace new experiences, to explore new frontiers. Like others in our culture, we were confident that we could be part of something new and better. In addition, because the call to renewal had come from the Church, the Pope and the bishops, we religious (obedient as always) took it very seriously and, I believe, were more affected by it than any other group in the Church was.[18]

While calls for a transformed and updated way of life for women religious came from the Cardinals in Rome, women responded because they wanted to participate in the broader culture. Catherine and the Sisters of Service were early witnesses to the possibilities of ministry and missionary work for willing and adventurous women. Catherine was not responding to a request from clergy when she proposed her ideas to Archbishop McNeil and Father Coughlan. There was *originality* in the impulse that moved her to consider a new way – one that brought together the gifts of the culture with the gifts of the tradition.

Catherine's innovations, realized in the life of the SOS community, pioneered in setting the history of Canadian women's religious communities on a new course. Even though the Vatican initially resisted the word *service*, regarding it as inappropriate in the name of a women's religious Institute, four decades later the council adopted the use of the term to communicate its new vision: "The church is not motivated by earthly ambition but is interested in one thing only – to carry on the work of Christ under the guidance of the holy Spirit, who came into the world to bear witness to the truth, to save and not to judge, to serve and not to be served" (*Gaudium et spes*). The SOS adopted a new integration in religious life for women – one that honoured their capacity for meaningful work in society with an equally meaningful role of servant leadership in the Catholic Church. Catherine's dynamic and active spiritual life of serving people in a rapidly changing world helps situate her in the movement for reform leading towards Vatican II. Dominican Sister Anne Marie Mongoven reflects on the quality of life in religious communities before Vatican II:

> The pattern of daily life was stable. I lived in a community of sisters in a convent located close to the parish church. Our community chanted the Office of the Blessed Virgin Mary each morning and each evening. We walked to church each day for Mass. Our daily schedule included time for meditation, spiritual reading, study, and recreation together. We ate our meals in silence, listening to spiritual reading at supper. We were teachers in the parish school. Life was prayerful. It had a daily rhythm.[19]

The SOS moved into dynamic new social roles as the Spirit made known the needs of others. After Vatican II, women religious stepped into public places where they developed their talents, skills and gifts to respond to the needs of the poor, the sick and the alienated. They also answered calls to study in universities and, eventually, to become professors themselves. Like Sister Brennan, Sister Mongoven speaks of the initiative of Pope Pius XII and Vatican II. As women obeyed the call for renewal of religious life, she says, "We had no idea where this obedience would take us, nor did the whole Church, including curial officials and the laity. Only the Spirit knew where we would be led."[20] Yet Catherine's direction towards a radical and innovative way of religious life did not mean she was abandoning her religious tradition. She sought to reinterpret the tradition of the Church in light of the particular problems she was facing in an entirely novel context. This, too, was a focus of Vatican II. Since the close of the council, communities of religious women have been one of the most outward signs of the reforms that were intended to lead the entire Church into service in the world.

Catherine and the SOS were part of a broader tradition of Canadian missionaries who, through daring and innovation, were able to adapt the Church's conventional ways of doing ministry, working without losing the "non-negotiables" of the Christian mission. Discerning what must remain and what could be changed in the traditional way of doing missionary work was a necessary practice for Catherine, and was an ongoing one throughout her life as a Sister of Service. As she often said, everything must be considered in light of need and feasibility. The big question was how the Church, in *this* place and *this* time, could answer the call of Christ as it responded to the needs of the poor and abandoned. Catherine demonstrated that she understood clearly the wisdom later to be given voice in the documents of Vatican II. The Church exists for the sake of the world, Vatican II taught, and not merely for the sake of its members.

Catherine's suggestions for reform in the new Institute of the Sisters of Service – long before Vatican II was convened – were taken into careful consideration by Archbishop McNeil and Father Coughlan. Many of these early reforms to religious life were so radical that traditionalists who placed great value on the external signs of commitment to religious life claimed that the SOS could not truly be called Sisters who lived in a Catholic religious community. A distinctive religious habit had been the most visible sign of a woman's status as a religious. For Catherine, this outward sign of commitment was not at the heart of women's religious identity. She decided the habit worn by traditional congregations was not suitable for the lifestyle of a frontier woman teaching long hours, ministering to the community at large and doing her own housework, cooking and laundry.

Catherine insisted from the very beginning on practical dress that would allow the Sisters to live in a fairly inconspicuous manner in frontier communities. In the first SOS missions, the Sisters would need to be able to move and work, even riding on horseback at times. Deeming the usual black and white habits impractical, she agreed that her Sisters could wear something akin to a nurse's uniform. A very practical sleeveless grey serge dress was designed, along with two pairs of attachable sleeves, white collars and cuffs and a matching grey serge hat. A small, simple silver cross on a blue cord was engraved on one side with the community's motto: "I have come to serve," and on the other side with the initials S.O.S. Sensible black oxford shoes completed the uniform. An ample cape was designed to wear in cold weather.

Catherine's views on designing a modified habit were insightful and practical, since in many missions the Sisters were so busy that it was difficult to find time even for the prayers and devotions that were required spiritual exercises for members of the community, let alone maintaining the more complicated habits worn by traditional nuns.

Other changes are reflected in the early Rules and Constitutions of the SOS, which, although startling to many, did not compromise the religious integrity of the Sisters. It was necessary, for example, to adjust the order of the day, known as the *horarium*. The Sisters arranged their days to include spiritual exercises, prayers, devotions, and Mass when available, but Catherine convinced Archbishop McNeil and Father Coughlan that the heavy religious and professional duties of the women would require good health and physical stamina, with enough sleep necessary to sustain them. The SOS therefore arranged a schedule to accommodate the demands of the missions as well as the spiritual practices of religious life in the community.

The frontier demanded further radical innovations. The Sisters often travelled alone, something not allowed in most communities of religious women. Great courage was needed to adapt religious life in these ways, since attention to the interior life of prayer and devotion would need to remain a central concern, even in the midst of the Sisters' busy lives. Could they be involved in these active and social ways and remain rooted in lives of prayer and contemplative awareness? Responsibility for spiritual nourishment and development began to rest more squarely on the shoulders of the women themselves, who cooperated in their missions to ensure their fidelity to lives of prayer and action.

The question of authority and obedience is an important one in any religious community. Although the Rules and Constitutions of the Sisters of Service outline the hierarchy of authority within the community, even in this matter there were allowances made for women to judge and decide for themselves in certain areas of life that were, for other religious communities, decided only by a religious Superior. Catherine's correspondence indicates that she seems to have enjoyed quite a bit of freedom in seeking out advice and in offering input about new missions – freedoms largely unavailable to most women religious prior to the post-council reforms.

These are just a few of the suggestions Catherine put forward in the beginning conversations about the SOS. Some of these changes set new trajectories for future religious life. These adjustments to conventional religious custom also indicate that at least some within the Church were willing to question the demands of rigid institutional rules. When Vatican II offered new insights into the self-understanding of the Church, it was because the bishops gathered up the wisdom of the faithful – people like Catherine – and offered a new interpretation that made Catholic tradition understandable and relevant in modern times. Accomplishing this shift in perspective meant considering the way the Church's life was being lived in the world. Among the topics for reflection at Vatican II was the Church's own need to learn new techniques, methods and types of ministry and missionary work.

The council relied on Revelation; what was refreshing was that Revelation was breaking down barriers between the Church and the world. It was also breaking down barriers within the Church itself. While this was not embraced by all – indeed, it was radically opposed by some within the Church – the new freedom being called for by the council was now formally part of the Church's own tradition. Catherine couldn't have been more pleased.

∾ Chapter Six ∾

A Spirituality of Liberation and Equality

The point of inclusion is the belief that each of us is important, unique, sacred, in fact. We can only relate to others and begin to include them in our lives and our society if we have this primary belief.

Jean Vanier, *Becoming Human*[21]

Catherine's worldview, her theology and her anthropology combined in a way that influenced her every feeling, thought, judgment and decision. Her biblically inspired images of God, her experience of God, her upbringing, her own reflections, her experience of community throughout different life phases – all reflected a fundamental theme: creation's unity seeking realization in the lives of creatures. The essential unity of God's creation was immediately recognizable for those who had eyes to see and ears to hear. The world was truly *in* God, as God was *in* the world. To strive spiritually is to strive for this perfect state of unity, possible only because God is the sovereign and supreme provider of all, for all. It was from this perspective – that of a whole creation made up of interrelated parts – that Catherine considered the question of human equality.

111

For Catherine, equality was a condition to be lived out in society as a witness to God's love and justice. When people experience inequality, they are tempted to adopt attitudes of inferiority or superiority, and Catherine opposed both. The Pauline influence in her spirituality supported her conviction that God intends every person to play an equally important role in the divine plan for creation. She would not accept a theology that allowed humans to adapt God's story to suit their own plans. Instead, she believed people are intended to discover how they fit into God's story – a story of love, unity and mutuality. Writing to Sisters Patricia Burke and Anna McNally, SOS, in 1979, Catherine reflected on the Missionary Oblates of Mary Immaculate (OMI Fathers), who observed the work of the Sisters of Service. This gave her an opportunity to explain the rationale:

> … experience at ground-level, and in the midst of the people, where reality can be seen by the human workers – This is the guide to God's Truth which is so necessary – the only truth – no guessing – no following of ancient ideas – of harmful old dug-in customs – no copying of old systems – except the virtues and what suits the SOS charism.

Catherine's disdain was reserved for customs that created division and competitive attitudes among people, while it is clear that she supported every aspect of the Church's tradition that promoted solidarity and attitudes of generosity among the people of God. The common perception of Roman Catholic nuns was that of a group of women "set apart" and sequestered within the mysterious walls of the convent. This situation restricted the women from the grassroots social work that Catherine saw as so important in building communities.

Also, too much emphasis on separateness got in the way of Christian solidarity in communities where people came from diverse religious backgrounds. Attempting to discourage divisiveness between Roman Catholics and Protestants, Catherine did not believe that the Church's teachings or its way of life should be used to separate Catholics from other Christians. Instead, she thought, Catholics should focus on the common aims of Christians and work together with others to build a unified country. This theological insight complemented her natural love of learning, making every environment a possible occasion for discovery of God's surprising presence.

At the time of the founding of the Sisters of Service, the women's suffrage movement had been ongoing in Canada, the United States and Europe from the mid- to late nineteenth century, creating powerful political undercurrents in North American society. Catherine admired those Canadian women who fought for women's rights in the late 1800s and the early decades of the 20th century. Due to their efforts, the legal status of women in Catherine's day was changed so that they could be considered persons under the law. As well, during the First World War, women, of necessity, moved into the public realm as workers, civil servants and military personnel, significantly altering some entrenched views about women's roles in society. Catherine was influenced by the prospect of new possibilities for women in civil service, and wanted to bring a new dimension of professionalism and public service to religious life.

In part, Catherine's plan involved transforming the prevailing culture in both Church and society. She hoped the work of women would come to be accepted in the realm of public service, since this was how women could bring their religious faith to life in the community. As she grew older, she was able to situate herself within women's history of emancipation from structures of domination and oppression. She knew that she and her Sisters had played a role in the struggle for equal rights for women both in Canada and in the Catholic Church.

While Catherine often expressed regret that the Church was still out of step with contemporary attitudes towards women's capabilities and leadership skills, she was proud of the efforts of some Church leaders to rectify the situation. During the 1960s, her letters frequently mentioned Cardinal Suenens, a leading voice at the Second Vatican Council, as just one of many Church leaders who saw the wisdom of addressing the root problems leading to restriction of women's roles within the Church. When Sister Lena Renaud was granted extraordinary ministerial privileges to attend to the spiritual needs of the parishioners at Camp Morton, Catherine believed she was seeing the dawn of women's equality in the Church.

Catherine argued for her authentic place in the Institute, in the Church, in society and in history – but she did more than that. She sought to change conditions that had supported and led to further inequality among people. She was not only concerned about equality for women, but desired the equality of all members of the Church, which meant reforming those aspects of the clerical system that supported notions of the superiority of clergy over religious women and the laity. She knew that the question of the equality of men and women in the Church was part of a larger problem. North American society was beginning to reform patriarchal systems of entitlement that Catherine perceived to be unjust and outmoded. Women's intelligence, in her mind, was unjustly ignored – especially concerning ideas and suggestions for social improvement and ministerial initiatives. She was often surprised and shocked by the gap between her expectations of equal treatment and her experiences of injustice. For example, Catherine wrote to Archbishop Henri Routhier in 1968 to explain her disappointment when her motives and actions were not taken seriously and no attempt was made to understand them. She described how she had worked to "study conditions" in Saskatchewan, taking an analytical and constructive approach to creating a model for missions. Her disappointment came when she realized that Father Daly misunderstood what she was proposing and working towards.

Catherine's vision of ministry was shaped by her experience of struggle, poverty and spiritual malaise among the people of the West. Immigrants from a variety of places landed together in these remote outposts, needing the strength that came from a common spiritual bond to forge their disparate families into a unified society. Catherine believed that the best spirit for this ministry was one that was entirely ecumenical and practical. In an account of SOS history, she wrote, "People who live very far away from where the stress or neglect exists and are never in the very midst of it, fail to be inspired in the right direction." Her insight and inspiration had been born in the milieu of the rural public school, which for her seemed to serve as a base in the community from which spiritual outreach could occur in a systematic way. This was a perspective from the ground up, or as it is sometimes called, "doing theology from below."

Although he and Catherine agreed on many things, especially that the Catholic Church in Canada needed to find a way to make itself present to Catholics in western Canada, Father Daly's understanding of the best approaches to western missions was, in many ways, vastly different from Catherine's. He often advised sisters to "Look at the Big Maps," a phrase that he had framed and hung in his Toronto office at the Motherhouse. He gained knowledge of the problems in the West while he was rector at Holy Rosary Cathedral in Regina from 1915 to 1918, and wrote about the issues facing the Catholic Church in his 1921 book *Catholic Problems in Western Canada*. His associations with prominent and influential people as he established the Catholic Truth Society – a Catholic organization committed to publishing and distributing materials about the faith and teaching of the Catholic Church – and in his extensive travels broadened his perspective and made his approach to missionary work very complex. His activities and associations sometimes caused him some problems with his superiors in the Redemptorist community, since his outgoing personality and love of modern technology were at times seen as incongruent with his vows of poverty and humility.

Father Daly's writings attracted the attention of Archbishop Neil McNeil and Father Arthur Coughlan. His vision and approach to making the Church more visible and active in the West answered the need to provide care and support for the vast numbers of immigrants arriving in Canada. This resonated with Archbishop McNeil's own desires and aspirations. Each of the people interested in founding the new community, including Catherine, believed that inaction on the part of the Church was to blame for failures to meet the needs of Catholics on the western frontiers of the developing nation. Each of them advised action that would be public, visible and effective in both religious and civic development.

Father Daly, in drafting the SOS rules and customs in 1922, described the approach of a Catholic presence mediated through teaching, nursing, catechetical instruction and social work. The SOS mission field was to extend from the ports in Atlantic Canada where the immigrants landed to the homesteads they built in the far reaches of the West. Father Daly's responses were to significant problems facing the Church in Canada, and went far beyond the scope of Catherine's original vision, which was limited to the western provinces and isolated rural areas.

The small missions Catherine envisioned required grassroots social cooperation with government, local school boards and all community members, all of which were possible for women in the teaching, nursing and, later, social work professions. In later years, according to Catherine, Father Daly admitted to her that he had not understood the public school system and policies that offered a unique opportunity for religious women to teach in these schools in the western provinces. Even though Catherine and Father Daly differed in their ideas about how to approach the problem of developing missions, her original idea continued to thrive within the overall thrust of the community's missionary endeavours. It should be noted that at the time of Father Daly's death in 1956, fourteen of the SOS's 32 missions were small teaching missions in western Canada.

Transformation of the Church's social structures, Catherine believed, would come as the Church adapted to the new social climate. She saw women participating in political and professional life, coming to know their own value and worth as persons who played a role in God's creative plans for the betterment of their world. She expected the Church, likewise, to open up pathways for women to participate in new positions of responsibility and leadership. As Catherine got older, she expressed her dismay at how naive she had been in assuming these changes would come easily. Writing to Sister Agnes Dwyer, she stated, "I was not mature in my knowledge of human nature – of the influence of chauvinism and desire for leadership. Though Faith was strong in me it ought to have been stronger." In a letter to Sister Patricia Burke, however, she expressed her conviction that whatever roles women came to play in the Church, they would be characterized by compassion, evolving under the inspiration of the Holy Spirit. She did not necessarily believe, however, that this would mean women would enter into clerical roles.

In 1966, Catherine explained that her own life was an example of how men and women were equal in the eyes of God. Reflecting on her first years of teaching and the responsibility she had assumed for her family, she shared her thoughts about the situation of women in the Catholic Church:

> The pressure for 'blind obedience' during that year, even in my ideas which had started the SOS (had given it a purpose entirely its own – had made its founding a must) staggered my trust in holy religious. They were conscientious victims of centuries of a philosophy which is no longer honored. Many of the clergy and many good women at that time still believed that the female of the species could be nothing but inferior – only second-class.

> If that were true – and it certainly was not – then the family challenge which my Heavenly Father had arranged for me when I was just grown to adulthood was fit for a man only. But such minds as those of John XXIII and Cardinal Suenens recognize and defend the truth that women are truly and undeniably on a par with men.

Catherine typically looked to her experience as the material for her reflections. She concluded that it had not been enough simply to put herself forward as a responsible person who hoped and desired to participate in the mission of the Church. She recalled that, to achieve the right to pursue her particular vocation, she had also resisted certain customs and traditions in the Church.

Existing models of leadership within the Church exhorted males to assume positions of authority and females to submit obediently to their leadership. Catherine always feared that the SOS was in danger of being lured back into the outdated philosophy and methods of those people she named "arch-conservatives," yet Canadian society and culture, she perceived, were beginning to reflect a growing acceptance of women's equality with men. Courageous women were embracing new opportunities for leadership through responsible social and political participation. Still, the Church's attitude, favouring clerical control, especially affected women's religious communities. Problems persisted because of the prevailing myth that women were inferior to men. Catherine saw the matter differently. Writing to Sister Madge Barton in 1969, she said,

> Now, Sister, 'man is man' not God. And all of us are 'the Church' as part of the Church, each of us ought to respond to the needs we see with our own eyes and experience. Do not wait for some human being to push you – some human being who is no more a part of the Church than you are. No Bishop has any right to think he knows why the SOS started, what was its need or is so today without deep investigation.

Catherine believed her resistance, as well as her constructive work, were validated in later years. She was conscious of the powerful spiritual forces at work within the Church's life as older conventions shifted and the Church struggled to liberate itself from bias and prejudice towards women. Heartened by the writings of people like Cardinal Suenens, Gregory Baum and Hans Küng, she was convinced the Church would, in time, correct the emphasis on male entitlement and accept the equality of Catholic men and women.

Catherine's opinion on women's ability to take on roles of public and religious responsibility was shaped by her own experiences. During her early years of teaching and travelling as a Sister of Service, two movements active in the West would influence Catherine's spiritual path. One was the women's movement for equal rights; the other was a complex political movement concerned with social and economic development.[22] In the West, as these movements converged, conditions were ripe for a new kind of women's religious endeavour – one that would liberate women from conventional restraints and allow them the freedom to be involved in creative and cooperative social ministry. Socially, conditions were favourable for fostering cooperation among the farmers and rural settlers who had unique social and economic concerns. Drawn to these movements, Catherine's concern was that they be supported and guided by an active Christian faith.

There was a place opening up for Catholic leadership, and Catherine realized women were well situated to take advantage of unique opportunities presented in the West. Schools and hospitals were among the first social institutions developed in rural Canada. Women who were professionally and spiritually prepared for this special work would be welcomed into the lives of settlers at early stages in the growth of their communities. She regarded teaching, nursing and social welfare work as very specific forms of leadership for women – professions that, by their very nature, would keep SOS close to the developmental roots of the community's life. The goal of such work was to foster mutual responsibility in a developing society, beginning with the children.

For someone like Catherine, who wanted to serve the Church in an active missionary role, marrying or entering cloistered religious life were limiting options. Professional career development among women religious in the Catholic Church was considered extraordinary. Increasingly, however, Canadians had been hearing from women like Nellie McClung, who resisted the domestication and privatization of their gender. Catherine applied this resistance within the Church when, in the early 1920s, she proposed her radical new way of religious life for women. Ultimately, Catherine merged her professional life of teaching with her religious vocation – not for personal satisfaction or social security, but because the needs of others called upon her to do so. Her desire to integrate her social aspirations with her religious ones meant crossing multiple boundaries in both Church and society.

As Catherine went out into the workforce as a member of a religious community, she was able to embrace that aspect of Catholic teaching on social justice that holds that poverty wears the face of Christ. It is a theme with deep biblical roots. Helping new Canadians integrate and participate cooperatively in social development therefore had a theological basis for Catherine. Understanding that the experience of poverty among Canadian immigrants, besides being a threat to sustaining life, was an experience of shame and social alienation, Catherine wanted to encourage Catholics to take up their social responsibilities. As she recognized, one aspect of salvation is that participation in the Body of Christ restores the lost to human dignity.

The needs of the poor moved Catherine's heart with Christ-like concern: charity, mercy, compassion, care and generosity. While she was concerned about the survival of Catholicism in Canada, she did not believe interreligious conflict or separatism were appropriate responses to the crisis facing the Church. She was convinced it was possible to influence development of healthy religious attitudes at the grassroots. Catholics could be examples of religious integrity as well as models of cooperation and acceptance in their diverse communities. Because the people of the West were poor, the women of the SOS would model equality and mutual responsibility among neighbours while living in poverty. This way, they might become examples for others. Taking the vow of poverty for spiritual reasons, and not as an end in itself, the Sisters' solidarity with the poorest and most abandoned in society was endowed with the purpose of inspiring others through their faith and action.

Generosity and compassion among the poor was truly evidence of God's love in the struggling communities of the West. Catherine's strategy was based on her understanding that there was liberating power in people's discovery of their own compassion, generosity, self-sacrifice and empathy. She wanted the people to recognize *themselves* as Church, but not in such a way that they came to identify with a social institution offering exclusive privileges of membership. She did not want Catholics to assume a position of superiority over others in the community. Catholics were to be at the service of the whole community, beginning with the poorest and most marginalized.

Reflecting on her life, Catherine described her experience of the changes to religious life that had occurred in her lifetime, especially concerning women's capacity to accept public roles in social and religious leadership. In 1972, she proposed a contrast between "two worlds":

1. There was the old world of Custom, blind obedience to it – just follow the boss' mind – a man's mind – females were definitely in the class of puppets and satisfied to be so – mostly.

2. But a New World had been born and was fighting for life and growth. Its helpers were Logic, Science, Faith.

Catherine demonstrated a remarkable openness to adaptation, and an enthusiastic willingness to bring new discoveries to life in religious work. Her way of living out her faith in public deserves a great deal of exploration. To this day, women struggle to transcend the limitations of cultures that place them in exclusively domestic roles or in very limited public roles. In Catherine's experience, women who fought for the right to live out their vocations in public ran the risk of social disapproval. For a significant part of her life, she was a member of a society that would not allow her to vote or to hold public office. Yet she participated in one of the greatest revolutions of our times, as women agitated for political and social reforms to allow them to participate fully in the public life of the nation. As the intellectual and moral equals of males, she believed that women could bring special qualities of care and nurturing into their work and influence the intellectual, moral and religious development of the people they served.

Catherine felt as though she was forced by her life circumstances to assume a public persona and that God had arranged this as her destiny. For example, she believed God had arranged the circumstances of her early life to compel her to take on roles normally reserved to males. She assumed it would be illogical for God to expect her to act in public ways outside the norm for her gender if God did not favour equality between males and females. Drawn to teaching and compelled to support her family, responsibility took her into the public domain rather than pressing her to conform to more conventional cultural stereotypes – the married woman, the spinster or the cloistered nun. She found the integration of the public life of a teacher with a religious vocation was a way for women to become leaders in the development of both Church and society. Supported by two pillars of learning and practice, Sisters of Service were professionals, called forth by the needs of their societies for education, health care and social welfare. They were also religious women of service, called to foster growth in the faith of Canadians on the frontiers of a developing nation. It was Catherine's original insight concerning the unique possibilities present in the western context that led her to suggest this integrated approach, setting a new course for religious life in Canada.

Catherine Donnelly with some members of the congregation after Mass in the Cariboo region of British Columbia, 1934.

Chapter Seven

A Spirituality of Cooperation and Development

I am about to do a new thing;
now it springs forth, do you not perceive it?
I will make a way in the wilderness
and rivers in the desert.

Isaiah 43:19

Catherine acknowledged the vital importance of a spirit of gratitude in religious life, often signing her letters with the phrase "In Gratitude" as an expression of the great value she placed on her relationships with others. This knowledge, and the spiritual disposition that it fostered, endowed her with love and appreciation of the relationships in her life. She came to view the friendship and mutuality that existed between the Sisters and the settlers as part of the Sisters of Service (SOS) mission. This approach is illustrated in a story that describes a gift that she and another Sister received while they were travelling the Cariboo region of British Columbia in the mid-1930s.

She and Sister Irene Faye had been visiting settlers from morning until night, travelling slippery roads in a torrential rainstorm. They expected to spend a miserable night at their makeshift campsite, which would surely have been damaged by the storm. When they arrived back at their camp, however, they were greeted by their hosts, the family that owned the land upon which they had camped. She described their experience in a letter to Toronto:

> As we approached our trees we saw that there was nothing left but the canvas roof and the hole in the ground and Mrs I. our hostess, was running towards us from her house.
>
> 'We have fixed up the milk-house for you. We cleaned it out and packed the cracks with moss and there's a stove and a fire on.' Blessed news! We made for the place in haste. I sat and gazed at the glowing stove for an hour at least. I wanted to make sure it wasn't only a dream. It was such a beautiful stove, the most delightfully handsome one I ever saw. The end door and the front door are all smashed and wired up. A flat piece of rusty iron does for the top where you put in the wood. It has only three legs and is white with age for it has seen so much 'Cariboo' life. Its red pipes are decorated with holes and rusty frilled edges. As the cold rain teemed down outside, I sat close to that thing of loveliness and comfort, the gift of the warm hearts of its owners. The red coals popped out of the holes in the broken front and lay glowing with hospitality and welcome on the little iron platform. Our host brought in a sheep skin and laid it on the clay floor in front of the fire, for our feet. The family were delighted that we appreciated their efforts so much.

As Catherine spoke of the people placing the sheep skin on the floor for their feet, she suggested that something was happening here between the Sisters and the settlers that had evoked the Christian spirit of service. Catherine surely appreciated the spiritual value of this gesture, which is reminiscent of Jesus bending to wash the feet of his disciples. Attitudes of generosity and welcome – the desired outcomes of Christian ministry – were being called forth by the presence of the Sisters. She understood what a gift this was for herself as a missionary. Her response was gratitude, a witness of thankfulness that showed a capacity to receive as well as to give. In her many descriptive accounts of acts of generosity, Catherine witnessed to the presence of those gifts of the Spirit that she believed to be the raw materials of genuine Christian community – compassion, generosity of heart and spirit, welcome and friendship. Telling stories like this one was her way of offering evidence of the success of the missions.

In her religious life, Catherine truly lived in some of the most impoverished conditions this country has ever known. The vow of poverty taken by the Sisters was not merely a way to achieve personal sanctity or spiritual perfection. The SOS charism of service meant that commitment to the vows of chastity, obedience and poverty ultimately freed them to focus on the needs of other people. Sisters had many opportunities to express gratitude for the generosity of others, since they participated in the economies of the communities as one aspect of their mission. As a missionary, Catherine was intensely concerned with local grassroots development, guided by her knowledge that "God provides!"

Throughout her life as a Sister of Service, Catherine consistently promoted her vision that large numbers of western public schools could become bases for the outreach and service of the SOS. The rural teaching missions were, for her, the daring outward expression of the spirit of the Institute. Confronting what she saw as a trend towards city work that had become the central focus of the SOS, she argued in a letter to Sister Madge Barton in 1966,

> You know how anxious I am to leave no stone unturned in regard to the schools. It is difficult for me to understand why so many people seem to think that city work or work like separate schools belongs to our spirit. It crept in because so many who were admitted were not schooled enough to attain professions. Rural teaching, health work and welfare work, fruitfully done, require professional training.

Clearly seeing the link between formation and mission, Catherine perceived that SOS work in public schools required a dynamic commitment to religious *and* professional work. In the 1920s, responding to such a challenge was a startling innovation in religious life. The mandate of the Sisters radically situated them in society, while the focus on western rural areas placed them on the margins, ministering among pioneers in isolated frontier settlements. The situation raised Catherine's consciousness of the need for Church reform. Her plan to foster healthy social development meant bringing together her biblically grounded Catholic faith and the best of promising modern achievements.

The SOS founders proposed strategic social positioning of religiously dedicated women as signs of the Church's presence in the wilderness. The people's poverty highlighted the need for just and compassionate social and economic reforms. Their ignorance in matters of Christian faith and Canadian culture called for evangelization and education. The spiritual challenges faced by settlers called for guidance and leadership, fostered through the gift of genuine Christian friendship. With sights set on the future, Catherine knew that persuasion would be most effective in the education of children: "All works of Religious Orders are good but none so potential as being WITNESS of God's Love and Peace and Justice among those of the growing generation which could quickly go very wrong and will be tomorrow's adults guiding nation and Church," she said.

Catherine's emphasis on professional development expressed her desire that SOS be formed as women sent forth to encounter people in the world. A public and socially interactive role for Sisters contrasted with the monastic norm, although many congregations of religious women established and worked in Catholic schools and hospitals. In the rural public school missions, the SOS worked in valued public institutions that were created through the shared efforts of all citizens. The Sisters interviewed for this book have all understood this spirituality to be at the heart of their SOS vocation, and feel connected to Catherine in their sharing of this spirit.

She urged Sisters to reflect upon the founding vision of the Institute, offering her insights about its key elements and foundations. Her emphasis increased at the time of Vatican II in the 1960s, when the large-scale movement of women religious from the convent into the public realm was in its infancy. She was conscious that SOS, begun much earlier in the same century, had taken its shape by radically altering many of the conventional norms for religious life among women. Indeed, the founding principles of the Institute resembled those that eventually supported instructions for reform in the Vatican II documents on the renewal of the Church and women's religious life. The motivation for the shift in the Church during Vatican II came from the Church's need "… to face the emergence of the behavioural sciences, as well as the increasing interdependence of the world."[23]

Catherine continually puzzled over the strong currents in the Church that stifled reform and threatened ecumenical advances. The need for professional development for women religious seemed obvious to her, but integrating professional commitments with those of religious life was a path along which the Church moved with great caution. Negotiating between the needs and possibilities present in the rural situations meant placing women religious right in the middle of social life. Since Catherine understood the development of spirituality and culture to be interrelated, integrating professional and religious life seemed like a logical step to her, and she dared to offer herself for service in both Church and society.

Her efforts took place against the backdrop of Catholic social documents, which expressed concern about the harmful consequences of liberalism and individualism, as well as the dangers of socialism. These documents began the Church's commentary on social order and justice in the modern world. On the one hand, the Enlightenment had elevated the worth and freedom of the individual; on the other, it brought into question the role of hierarchical authority in both Church and state. Alternatively, socialist philosophy criticized the unrestrained freedom of the individual. It argued against the injustice of a rich and greedy elite burdening large numbers of the working poor. In its most radical forms, socialism tended towards the subordination of the needs of the human individual to the needs of the state as a whole. In the context of the newly developing Canadian West, a clash of ideologies about social development left many people confused and created political tension.

At the dawn of the 20th century, competing worldviews challenged the generally accepted notion of social order embraced by most

Catholics. The frontiers of western Canada – a country in the making – were places of political, social and religious tension. Catherine wanted Catholic immigrants to participate in creating their societies, carrying forward the best of their traditions while learning how to promote the ideals of unity and solidarity. It was time for considering new philosophical, political and economic approaches to working out the relationship between the individual person and society. New ideologies sparked a variety of political and social movements. In countries where democracy had taken root, the general population was now responsible for deciding the fate of nations as they moved into the future. Citizens needed practical guidance and the gifts of memory and foresight as they discerned between different political and economic strategies. In the late nineteenth and early 20th centuries, popes began to speak directly about the social problems facing human beings.

With great foresight, Catherine identified the need to integrate faith and social development at the ground level, anticipating the reforms in Church thinking that eventually found a voice in the documents of Vatican II. She expressed, in practical ways, the Catholic Church's rising concern about social, political and economic development among the peoples of the world. Beginning at the local level, her vision expanded towards a global horizon. She shared the settlers' experiences of real poverty, political upheavals, and the rise of individualism and materialism. From her social location, she struggled to reimagine the relationship between Church and state, and the relationship of the human person to both.

Catherine's perception of the person and society, and her understanding of the dynamic relationship between them, was heavily coloured by the agrarian influences of her upbringing and by her Celtic spirituality. In the rapidly changing political climate of the early 20th century, she drew upon the wisdom of the traditional worldview she had inherited – one that evoked the ideal of the Middle Ages. She saw the world as a place of wholeness, health and goodness. In the idyllic image of that world, individuals found meaningful work valued by all, giving them the security of an integral place in the social order, albeit in terms of powerful hierarchies. People required the protection of beneficent governments that oversaw the common good and brought justice to the poor and oppressed. In his work *Catholic Social Teaching, 1891 – Present: A Historical, Theological and Ethical Analysis*, Father Charles Curran describes the worldview of many Catholics of Catherine's time:

> The Middle Ages epitomized the Christian ideal: the social person in an organic society. Liberalism, individualism, and selfishness did not exist at that time. All Christians were united in the one true Christian religion, which permeated the lives of everyone and the culture of the times. Kings and rulers recognized their obligation to God and to natural law. They served as defenders of the poor, the downtrodden, widows, and orphans. Social solidarity, as illustrated in the guild system, marked the economic organization of society. The guilds brought together everyone in a particular craft and worked for the good of all. The individualistic quest for wealth and personal gain did not exist; labor and work aimed primarily not at acquiring a personal fortune but at earning a comfortable living. The ideal was the small town surrounded by farm areas and presided over by the steeple of the church in the center of the town. There were none of the problems that the Industrial Revolution brought to the burgeoning cities of the late nineteenth century. Yes, such a society was hierarchical, static, and heavily agrarian, but in the eyes of many Catholics this was the Christian ideal.[24]

While Catherine held many of these traditional views about social development, she did not cling nostalgically to medieval notions of social order and custom. She was aware of the dynamic nature of social development and the emergent nature of societies.

In Canadian politics, systems that required personal responsibility and grassroots participation were replacing old world hierarchies of power and control. Catherine believed that these reform movements, including those begun in Luther's revolt against injustice in the Church, should also be taken seriously as spiritual movements. In her opposition to systems of privilege and entitlement in Church and society, she looked beyond Catholic social doctrine as it was being expressed in the nineteenth- and 20th-century social justice documents of the Vatican. That doctrine still professed that God endowed the monarchical systems of state government with authority, and that rulers should govern with "fatherly solicitude." For Catherine, the leadership of Pope John XXIII indicated a decisive shift from old ways of thinking to contemporary models of organizing society and Church. Speaking of the difficulty she had experienced in updating the technique and dress of the Sisters of Service, she mused in a 1965 letter to Archbishop Henri Routhier that papal authority had finally expressed support of the original SOS vision for a reformed Institute in the Church: "There was no John XXIII for backing in those days – but our spirit was ready all the way." Catherine was aware that political democracy offered opportunities for growth in responsible civic, moral and religious participation for all people. She wanted the Church to become involved in persuading this development to occur in ways that respected the moral and religious foundations of faithful Christian life.

The belief that intervening in the early stages of growth would influence development of the rural settlements complemented the ideals of democratic freedom and the responsibility of individuals. Theologically, this conviction challenged the top-down authority model of the monarchical systems endorsed by the Catholic Church. In advocating for freedom, equality and participation in developing societies, Catherine took a stance officially resisted by the Church hierarchy at the time. She perceived that each society and its social institutions really grew according to the ideals, values, resistances and biases of the founding members. Therefore persuasion, rather than dominating force, would most effectively influence social development. Since public schools were places where society employed persuasion most consciously, they seemed to Catherine to be the best locations for this type of constructive missionary work. Catherine chose to focus on matters related to grassroots development. She appealed to the common sense and goodwill of citizens instead of trying to apply abstract theories to practical situations. Her approach was illustrated in the advice she offered to other Sisters, stating, "Psychology shows us that the children are the ones who can be impressed – that will affect many generations to come, too. An ounce of living with children in an organized classroom is worth 1000 pounds of theory and high falootin talk." In the rural public school missions, Catherine considered the practical situations of settlers in light of their needs: for education, for fidelity to religious belief and practice, and for a strong moral foundation to guide community growth. A letter to Sister General Patricia Burke of the SOS in 1972 distinguished between the ivory tower approach to the Church's mission and the new Institute, which was "a determined and definite 'break-away' from old forms and decadent customs and completely false ideas about Christians as a whole." While she agreed it was important for Catholics to learn the doctrine of the Church, her approach to their needs was primarily pastoral and concerned with the interdependent development of people in healthy societies.

Remembering the experience of raising Mamie, her younger sister, Catherine thanked God for the presence of others who had helped in matters of morals and faith. In a letter to Sister General Patricia Burke in 1972, she reflected on the value of the community in early childhood development:

[Mamie] was where she observed good people and saw their life style and mingled with all kinds of pupils in an ordinary High School – but she saw the life-style of truly beautiful people and knew there were dangers. I know well what a tremendous influence a capable teacher can be and we must surely know that God wants help for all his children. What I have seen with my own eyes I must continue to believe.

This memory stayed with Catherine as she formed her plans for missionary work in the rural areas of the newer parts of Canada. The same principles and ideals would hold true in a general way for all children, regardless of their religious background.

Catherine realized that influential women could protect and guide the youngsters during the establishment and growth of new communities. Her strategy was to make the most of interpersonal encounters as opportunities to influence social dynamics in favour of responsibility and participation in Church and civic life. The moral and spiritual dangers that she knew were present in Mamie's experience existed in even greater proportion in the newly settled West. Catherine thought that a basic resistance to evil and immorality, complemented by a strong commitment to healthy development, would be necessary in the rural areas: "… the ideal work of the SOS is prevention of evil and construction of good." For pioneers, building social infrastructure – schools and hospitals, for example – was a practical necessity. Sharing institutions offered chances for different ethnic and religious groups to work together, but it also created tension and competition as groups sought to establish dominance within the new systems. Catherine believed, however, that it was possible to influence the development of this necessary infrastructure in favour of cooperation and social integration. She perceived that social institutions came into being as people organized their responses to real needs. Each community, therefore, was somewhat different and needed to be considered from the standpoint of local needs and local possibilities. Very early in the development of each community, the need for a school was always recognized. In this, she saw her opportunity to grasp the grace present in the situation.

Catherine stressed that the SOS's coordinated missionary efforts should radiate from the central hub of rural public schools. Subtly and sensitively, the SOS could "help to 'shape' the spirit or tone of the growing town." Responding to practical problems with a sense of urgency, Catherine did not set about creating complex theories about what to do. Her spirituality expressed itself in simple action, with her focus firmly set on mission and self-sacrifice. She established some basic principles for the work, assuming that a suitable spirituality would support the Sisters as practice in the field got under way. Her daring proposal for missionary work integrated the work of the Church and the work of the Canadian government in isolated rural outposts where efforts towards both religious and civic development were proving difficult.

The focus on urban societies left vulnerable settlers beyond the attention and outreach of the established Church in Canada, Catherine realized. "The people of the 'farming-West' are desperate," she wrote to Sisters Patricia Burke and Anna McNally. "The clergy of past years seem to see the crowds of people in the cities and large towns, get involved with them and have no time to go among the farm people." Concerned Catholics like Father Daly had tried for years to raise awareness that the problem facing the Church in the West was a problem facing the entire Roman Catholic Church of Canada. Large numbers of Catholic immigrants abandoned their own faith traditions in order to accept the helpful and accessible ministry of Protestant missionaries. Catholic leaders worried about the proselytizing efforts of Protestants, suspicious that their motivations stemmed from a desire to build a Protestant and English Canada. These fears arose as it became evident that many Catholic immigrants were relinquishing their faith traditions to assimilate into the dominant culture of their new home.

A few Catholic missionary priests and members of religious orders travelled the frontier territories, bringing what spiritual support they could to the struggling settlers. Most of these missionaries could barely provide for their own material needs. This outreach was woefully inadequate to the needs of the local Church, but given the realities of geography and the scarcity of willing missionaries, Church leaders were at a loss as to what to do.

In some areas of eastern Canada, a competitive attitude existed between Catholics and Protestants in local situations. Catherine hoped to avoid the development of such tensions, or at least to minimize the impact of these tensions on the progress of community development. Dedicated missionaries who worked among the people were most likely to appreciate the need for cooperation among all Canadian citizens in building and coordinating social institutions. As need drove people to transcend their fears of other groups, a more generous spirit prompted them to imagine new ways for Christians to cooperate in building their communities. Catherine emerged as a leader in this wave of innovative thinkers and actors. The possibility of spiritual renewal among the settlers encouraged her to look at the situation with eyes of faith.

In addition to their professional and religious roles, empathy and solidarity placed Sisters squarely within their social world. If the Institute's service was to be for all community members and not just for members of a select group, then a common social location that could serve as a central place of encounter would be required. Catherine knew from experience that teachers in rural public schools came face to face with the entire spectrum of the life of the community in their relationships with children. "All people in an area around an SOS centre, are regarded as legitimate claimants of our service," Catherine said. The rural public school was a place where she could make meaningful contact with the majority of the local population. The hope was that Sisters could subtly influence the settlers towards responsibility in matters of faith and justice. Learning to act in ways that lifted them out of poverty, the settlers could overcome exclusion, alienation and prejudice.

Showing a remarkable gift for appreciating the interplay between personal and communal faith and justice, Catherine demonstrated a strong desire to use her God-given gifts of reason and faith in assuming responsibility for judgments and decisions in social and ecclesial situations. She saw reform as a vital part of the Church's life and reasoned that those aspects of the Church's life that were manmade would always be in need of conversion. This led her to propose that her community step across social and religious barriers to embrace new ways of serving the poor, because God's love became known to human beings through an abiding presence that animated their lives.

Catherine's lively and socially oriented faith emerged from her understanding that the Church exists for the sake of the world. This *other-centred* spirituality set her free to serve the poor in a radical way. The most innovative aspect of Catherine's approach to serving the poor was that of using the fledgling public schools as a base from which to work. She believed that all children in a community should develop together in all developmental areas, including spiritually, as an integral part of their overall education program, regardless of their religious background. Her plan was to encourage Christians to work together and for Catholics to cooperate with those of other religious denominations for the common good. At the heart of her vision was the image of the Church turned towards the suffering of the world's people, compassionately and generously working for the growth of virtuous communities.

Working cooperatively with others included facing the social problems they shared, especially the scourge of poverty. This image – of the Church turned towards the poor – is often evoked in the testimony that settlers offered about the Sisters. During the Great Depression of the 1930s, the Sisters of Service missions were often the conduit through which generous donations of clothing, food, toys and books – most of which were collected and shipped through the Catholic Women's League, who supported the SOS in a number of ways – were distributed among the settlers of the struggling western provinces. From their unique social location within the rural public schools, the Sisters were able to discern the desperate needs of families because of their contact with their children.

Catherine's trusting faith in God's providence allowed her to seek beyond her own needs, knowing that God would provide all that was required in support of her dedication to the Gospel mission. Dismissing concerns about personal welfare, she wrote, "Anyway, worry does no good but strong Faith with all possible action added to Faith defeats the Devil. Evil has worked here through all the y[ea]rs here and has not quite defeated work for God here yet." She encountered her neighbours in the world as objects of God's concern, therefore, and set her focus on studying their situations and learning about their needs.

Catherine relied upon the inspiration of the Holy Spirit to help her understand the relationship between people's needs and what God was making possible. In her words, intelligence and eyes of faith could discern how to negotiate between "need and feasibility." The feasibility in each context was the concrete response to human need that God's grace made possible. This approach speaks of Catherine's openness to God's entry into human consciousness in the form of graced possibility. The same practical understanding of the need for discernment within particular social locations guided many of the reforms of Vatican II.

Catherine was confident God was working at subtle levels in the encounters of missionaries with the poor and the oppressed. The

Church's members would have to question and learn in different contexts to make Catholic faith relevant to the real needs of these people. Along with other Catholic missionaries of the 20th century, she spoke of respecting the power of the poor to enter into the work of creating their communities, an insight that began to be expressed in Latin America in the 1970s as liberation theology. Committed to basic Christian renewal, she argued that each community's spirit showed its own inspiration and initiative within the scope of its own local culture and economy. She interpreted Scripture and Church teaching as guides to social development, mindful that God commands the moral responsibility of human beings. In her *Man Alive* interview with Roy Bonisteel in 1980, Catherine spoke of the Ten Commandments as one of the directives she believed God had given her. Her concern for moral development was often a theme of her letters arguing for the program of missionary work in rural areas. She was guided by her insight that moral responsibility has social roots as well as social consequences.

As missionaries, the Sisters respected the freedom, creativity, dignity and desire of the settlers. The emphasis was placed on helping people become conscious of their need for God's sustaining power, while developing appropriate attitudes of attentiveness, reverence, gratitude and social cooperation. These attitudes would naturally permeate the social fabric of their communities. Catherine's theology of *encounter*, from its biblical roots to its public expression in human community, guided her approach to mission life on the frontiers.

Catherine did not expect people at the grassroots of society to seek unity through intellectual agreement about Christian dogma or doctrine. The question of Christian unity, to her, was grounded in humanity's need for God and community. The religious view of the world communicated through Scripture and tradition spoke of an *essential* unity, as a state of interrelatedness and wholeness given to creation by God. That is, humans share this world, whether or not they agree about anything. The question of unity, therefore, arose from the concrete experience of people's desires, practical needs, shared concerns and common human destiny.

Catherine observed and reflected upon the fundamentals of Christian action: "Humble kindness and knowledge of human nature and how to get down to the very grass-roots of social welfare work is what is needed." Constant prayer, solidarity, practical help and persuasive presence were the most effective paths to Christian solidarity. In formulating her questions about what to do, she adopted the point of view of the poor farmers who needed assistance. Her critical analysis of the situation included a critique of the Church. By asking about the institutional Church's capability to meet the need of its members in the way that she did, she was able to identify some obstacles hampering the Church's mission. Imaginatively, she worked out a new form of mission that was biblically grounded. This method respected the essentials of the tradition, but eliminated some of the obstacles and barriers that had formed along the lines of outdated customs. In a letter to Sister Patricia Burke from a mission in Northern Saskatchewan in 1979, Catherine wrote,

> The Northern parts of Manitoba, of Saskatchewan, of Alberta are our SOS vast field. Good women teaching in public schools, nursing, doing welfare work have impressed all kinds of people – families struggling in this rich soil land to form homes – ready to accept good teachers, nurses, welfare workers – people who get help in their desperation.

On the frontier, a practical and pastoral approach to Christian unity made the most sense. In situations of crisis, people *needed* to cooperate. Catherine saw this as an opportunity for pastoral guidance, helping people to consider their experience of need at the deeper level of spirituality. As we have learned in the current ecological crisis, consensus about theological and philosophical points takes a position of relative importance when considered against humanity's *need* to cooperate in projects that concern all human beings.

Catherine was empathetic towards farmers, and considered herself a farmer all her life, asserting, "I was born a farmer." However, there is more involved in understanding her missionary approach in the frontier settlements of the West. She wanted to protect a way of life that she sensed was in danger. As a person used to living close to the land, Catherine knew that the uniqueness of each family, each farming situation and each project of community development created a wealth of distinctions and differences that any missionary project would have to acknowledge. Political, social and economic dimensions unique to rural life would have to be taken into consideration. No one-size-fits-all approach could hope to meet the real needs of farmers. Although aware that the concerns of the Church were global, she stressed the need for the SOS to remain faithful to the Institute's original mandate. It was the activity of the Church and community in transforming local cultures that occupied Catherine's attention.

The Catholic Church faced great difficulty in responding to the often desperate needs of Canadian farmers in a drastically shifting economy and an unstable political climate. Pastoral care was required for their faith, and moral guidance was needed for the healthy development of their families and communities. Catherine's strong belief in cooperation and coordination between religion and state guided her action, while her *catholicity* expanded her outreach to include all citizens. The settlers' needs were universal and hence not exclusive to the Catholic population. She and other Sisters who worked in the rural missions made a choice to join their destiny to that of Canadian rural dwellers of all religious faiths.

During the 20th century, industrial growth was claiming the attention of the majority of Canadian people. The growth of urban centres was associated with technological growth and progress. Seemingly miraculous inventions appeared to be leading the way to a utopian future – a vision that fuelled the materialistic fervour of a rapidly developing population of consumers. The agrarian way of life was coming to be regarded by some as an outmoded and backward lifestyle – but it was a way of life that Catherine believed was essential to the future of Canadians. In 1948, she expressed concern that some manner of preserving the farming way of life was necessary to offset the loss of young people to the cities. Some years later, it was evident that she still perceived the need to speak on behalf of rural citizens. In a 1969 letter to Sister Patricia Burke, Catherine wrote,

Always (not just of recent years) the rural people have become discouraged and moved to the cities to add to the slums there. This is why SOS should make a drive to help more to make rural life worth while – to show families how to be happy there, to deal with gov[ernment] officials in behalf of rural life. This can be done.

As Catherine was figuring out a way to respond to the plight of farmers and rural settlers, the Church was recognizing that industrialization and urbanization posed significant challenges to sustaining ways of life associated with farming and basic industry – the way of life of the majority of people in the world. The agrarian way of life was giving way to the rapid growth of cities, drawing people from the country to work in developing industries and specialized professions. In truth, many urban dwellers lived in dire poverty, were unemployed or worked for unjust employers. The Church decried the loss of meaningful and productive work, urging human beings to recover their sense of personal agency in society.

Catherine believed that SOS teachers, health care workers and social workers in rural districts could convince farmers of the value of agricultural work, helping them to find joy and a sense of accomplishment in their way of life. Just as she hoped to prevent the leakage of Catholics who drifted away from the Church, she also hoped to prevent the leakage of farmers who drifted to the cities in search of prosperity and happiness. She struggled to reinterpret the role of Catholic faith in meeting the new challenges of the times in agrarian communities. Often working in pairs or in small groups, the Sisters dared to offer themselves fully in the far-flung and isolated places of the West, without substantial resources or support from the Church. This work required radical trust in God's providence – trust that helped them sacrifice their desire for the comfort and gifts of an established Church. As Catherine said, "We have only God! And His ways of providing for us are indeed marvellous."

Catherine often cited the Gospel of Luke, reminding others that Christians must "render to Caesar the things that are Caesar's and to

God the things that are God's" (Luke 20:25). For her, this teaching offered evidence that civic responsibility was a foundational dimension of the Christian life. The joining of the two – civic life and the commitment of the Christian to God's reign – meant that these dimensions of life should be in dialogue with one another in each person's life. As Catherine said, this was a path that required both cooperation and resistance. The Christian was required to be "wide awake."

Catherine fully engaged the culture of her world. In the 1980 *Man Alive* program, when Roy Bonisteel asked whether God spoke to her, she replied that God told her to "get on the right track." Significantly, she referred to divine authority to assert her personal right to judge and to choose her path, thus demonstrating her conviction that God desires humans to decide how they will give value to the things of this world in light of their faith and religious understanding. This stance also marked her disposition towards religious life. She believed Christians could develop the intelligence, emotional maturity and faith required to discern the significant religious questions facing them, and to grasp the possibilities before them as responsible human beings in history.

Conscious of the relationship between spirituality and culture, Catherine advised other Sisters of Service about how to engage the cultures of new missions: "Start [SOS] communities for places where you see the need and shape them to suit that particular culture – that atmosphere, the kind of feasibility in that location which has appealed to your spirit." Each SOS mission, therefore, would be a unique expression of spirit, and a broad range of SOS missions would honour the diversity of God's creation. She looked within the culture of a particular place and people for signs of how God's grace invited action. Religious sensitivity to culture meant respect for the unique and local interrelationships of the people with their land and with one another. This made missionary action a matter of discernment, an action of cooperating and coordinating effective service in collaboration with others. This attentiveness to local realities meant taking the wisdom of the people into account, evoking their genuine spirit instead of imposing a certain expression of spirituality upon the community.

Catherine enthused about the new theology entering discussions during her lifetime about the Church's mission in the world, particularly during the 1960s focus on Vatican II. The influence of a number of theological experts resulted in new teachings about the Church's life in the world, and generated greater interest in developing the Church's theology of the Holy Spirit. This theological development attracted Catherine, whose personal theology had, more and more, come to focus upon the activity of the Holy Spirit in the world. During this time, Catherine came to see herself as one of many Catholic social activists whose work had influenced the Church. She frequently expressed her enthusiasm as her Church became increasingly involved in social development, paying particular attention to social justice.

In many ways, the radical shifts that took place at the time of Vatican II validated Catherine's early beliefs and actions as a religious woman. She pointedly referred to the connection between her early ideas and the developments taking place at the time of the council, and clearly indicated that the roots of these developments were spiritual, as she expressed in a 1966 letter to Sister Madge Barton:

> … after I had done difficult and disappointing research work on my own initiation and with some suggestions from Fr A[rthur] Coughlan, we found this Western rural work impossible without the organization of an entirely new Order with a very different spirit – really the spirit of Pope John [XXIII] which was to awake the world decades later.

Among these shifts was the Church's updating of its understanding of itself and its relationship to other churches and religions. Throughout the development of Christianity, Christians have encountered difficulties in opening themselves to relationships with those outside their boundaries. Catherine's proposals for action in ministry, as well as her personal embrace of those with other religious affiliations, identify her as a person of ecumenical orientation, one of those leading the wave of new attitudes within the Church.

During the course of Vatican II, the Church shifted its thinking on a number of essential matters. There were many reasons for these changes. Church leaders were listening to what was being learned from the movement of the Spirit as it was being revealed in the lives of the Church's members. As well, theologians were systematically present-ing theories about the theology that guided innovative ministries, and proposing new ways of understanding the meaning and significance of such thought. The council was a reinterpretation of the Church in the face of contemporary challenges – but in itself it was a revelation that the Church continues to receive the teaching of the Holy Spirit and so must itself be open to revelation through its encounters with God in the world.

One of the greatest shifts in the life of the Church that took place at this time was the Church's understanding of its own mission. In *Compassion and Solidarity: The Church for Others*, theologian Gregory Baum (who was present at the council as a *peritus*, or expert) speaks of the intention to shift the focus of the Church's attention, especially in the document *Gaudium et spes* (The Pastoral Constitution on the Church in the Modern World):

> In this document the Church defined itself as sent into society as friend and servant. It is the Church for others. Its task is to bear the burden with other people, to struggle with others for greater justice, and to strengthen the bonds that unite people, despite differences in religion, culture, and racial origin, and in doing so to become conformed to its Master who came to serve, not to be served.[25]

Catherine's theology, while pre-dating this shift, fell along these lines, as it focused on Jesus' inclusive, healing, forgiving and other-centred ministry to those he encountered in his society – regardless of their ethnicity, religion or social status.

As with other ecumenists, Catherine was influenced by her en-counters with non-Catholic Christians. Among those moved with compassion and animated with a desire for justice on behalf of all people, this spirit of generosity towards others exerted a strong influ-ence within the Church at the time of Vatican II. According to Baum, this spirit signalled a change in the Church's attitude: "Christians of our day have begun to realize the destructive historical consequences of the Church's traditional exclusiveness ... Because of its narrow view of God's grace, the Church was unable to extend its solidarity to outsiders."[26] Catherine's challenge to this attitude reflected her conviction that the Church should strive to imitate the expansive and inclusive love of God for creation.

Catherine's economic vision for the SOS reflected the integrity of her vision. Although she adopted a very precise argument resisting outside funding of the Institute in its missionary work in the West, obviously she did not know what the future would hold, or how theologians would eventually be able to explain the liberating aspects of God's presence in light of contemporary global economic concerns. Yet her foresight in this matter, partially shaped by her Pauline spirituality, was evident in her plan to work with local economies, especially in the earliest phases of their development. When the Sisters moved into communities to teach, nurse and engage in social welfare work as professionals, their services would be paid for by the people's taxes. Citizens of the local community would therefore be accepting the Sisters, who would live among them in very practical and sustainable ways. The rural work of the SOS, as she explained it to Sister Patricia Burke in 1979,

> could include all kinds of help for families as the regular school work provided a salary responsible for provision by all the people served – wages shared in the providing, by all the families. All Canadians shared in the benefits given by devoted, dedicated teachers. All denominations should share in the salary-providing. That was my idea. All got the service, all should pay. It was service to the nation – a national endeavour.

Although this approach was bound to raise some concerns among the majority of Protestants in the West, people in the rural areas would know that they contributed to the Sisters' welfare through their taxes. Catherine believed that as all citizens came to value the contributions of the Catholic Sisters, they would view this relationship as one of mutual support and benefit.

In Catherine's vision, the Sisters and those in their missions were to be economic partners. This practical basis for relationship meant two things: first, the Sisters themselves would be made to satisfy the general criteria for suitability in their professions. This would do much to reduce the suspicions and divisions that often arose in communities of Catholics and Protestants. Second, the SOS would agree to accept wages that reflected the realities of local economies, and at times to suffer along with the people when there was no money to pay for services vital to the life of the community. As Catherine expected, it was this solidarity with the people, even when the Sisters could not be paid, that earned them respect and love in the places where they worked.

❧ Chapter Eight ❧

A Spirituality of Hope and Endurance

The saving journey of Jews and Christians is marked by long experiences in a hostile desert and a bruising exile, by a painful way of the cross. If harmony and calm are worthy goals, the path that leads to these ideals is most often marked by struggle and conflict.[27]

James and Evelyn Whitehead

atherine Donnelly experienced conflicts and trials as part of her human journey. Naturally, she responded emotionally to what hurt or threatened her. Anger, sadness, frustration and loneliness have often been considered obstacles on the spiritual journey, and in Catherine's life these human experiences were woven into the very fabric of her existence. The struggle she experienced between healthy detachment and emotional engagement raises the question of the role of emotions in spirituality. By expressing the emotions associated with her pain, longing, anger and grief, it may have seemed Catherine was having trouble accepting God's will. The role of the passions in spirituality has long been a matter of debate in the Christian tradition. James and Evelyn Whitehead ask us to consider some important questions about the full range of human passions in spirituality: "Is anger a natural enemy of spirituality? Are grief and loneliness distorted emotions that jeopardize our life of faith? Or are these painful stirrings wellsprings of our vitality, alerting us to endangered values and linking us to this passionate God?"[28]

Catherine's spirituality, with all of its passion, its emotion, recalls the age-old wisdom that even in the face of great obstacles and struggles there is reason to believe that good will prevail over evil – that the human condition leads towards hope and not towards despair or meaninglessness. Only the most pessimistic of philosophers have abandoned this hope in their attempts to speak about the future that lies beyond the crises we encounter in our lives. Catherine followed her patron, St. Paul, by advocating and modelling full emotional engagement in the struggle to live for God and to resist evil.

The frequent bouts of anger and frustration that others witnessed in their encounters with Catherine suggest she avoided an overly idealistic spirituality in favour of one respectful of real experiences of pain and suffering. She sought ways to reconcile the adventure of the religious quest with the experience of suffering in her life, even though at times her agitation led to emotional suffering and strains upon her relationships with others. Her path towards holiness was one of both joy and anguish. Writing to another Sister, she advised, "Be fearless – it is lots of fun! satisfaction! – a kind of suffering which leads to Heaven."

The Whiteheads label anger as "a revolutionary emotion." Considered in this way, it is possible to seek out the positive place of some of the anger and conflict in Catherine's spirituality. At times anger appeared to lift Catherine out of depression, prompt action for change and lead her away from despair. The explanations and insights of the Whiteheads can help us to understand how Catherine's anger was, at times, what Aquinas saw as "a just vindication, rather than indiscriminate revenge." Careful study of Catherine's expressions of frustration, anger, disappointment and grief reveal that much of her passion expressed her desire for justice. Her energy was usually directed towards her goals of transformation and renewal in the Institute, instead of blaming or vilifying others in a vengeful way.

In Catherine's later years, anger surfaced because of her conflicts with others regarding the directions taken by the Sisters of Service (SOS). During that time, she experienced intense emotional responses to the indignity she had felt in not being taken seriously within the SOS, and disillusionment because of the Institute's inability to realize the original vision she had shared with Father Coughlan. Certainly, religious formation as she experienced it would have persuaded her to suppress and deny her anger and frustration, to use these experiences as ways of uniting with Christ in his passion. This may have resulted in a complacent attitude towards the development of her Institute – and this certainly would not have been possible for Catherine. Anger energized her to seek reform and to rectify injustice for the good of all. One explanation for this justice-seeking attitude is that Catherine took her emotions seriously. Her Creator was the creator of human emotion, a sign of God's concern for earthly existence with all of its trouble, pain and turmoil.

Prayer and presence were Catherine's consolation. In prayer, Catherine sought practical support from God, as well as from those who had already gone to be with God, rather than seeking spiritual consolation divorced from the suffering in this world. She believed that work, prayer and hope were integral human activities for those who hoped to engage the spiritual life in ways that mattered in this world. Her consolation was the awareness that God was with her in her suffering, as well as in her moments of joy. She discovered signs of God's presence in the love of her family and friends, in nature and in the joy of growing things. These encounters convinced her that glimpses of heaven, our hope of union with God, were foretastes of the eternal life awaiting us. As on earth, Catherine's Heaven was a place of community and communion, a place of understanding and knowledge – even a place of continued learning.

Catherine followed the biblical tradition, believing that in the cosmic struggle between the power of light and the power of darkness, God would prevail. In her Bible she underlined a passage in the Book of Job that speaks of God's mysterious power to bring evil to light and to overcome it with divine justice. Job 12:22 reads, "He uncovers the deeps out of darkness, and brings deep darkness to light." She experienced the crises in her own spiritual life as part of this struggle between darkness and light, at times succumbing to stress and occasionally to despair. By the time she reached middle age, a variety of teaching and missionary experiences had been woven into a rich tapestry of life: friendships, losses, conflicts and professional accomplishments. Catherine began to focus her efforts on agitating among the Sisters, trying to convince them of the validity of her original vision and even going so far as to consider breaking away and beginning a new community.

By 1940, Catherine's role in the founding of the Institute was little known among the Sisters of Service. The Sisters acknowledged Father Daly as the founder and principal organizer of all the activities associated with the community's nationwide network of ministries and missions. Working constantly in the missions for over a decade, Catherine had not had many opportunities for rest and refreshment, nor did she have time to pursue her professional goals or her dream of finishing her university degree. Her desires took second place to the practical needs of the settlers and of the Institute. As she explained it in 1966, in a letter to Sister Marge Denis, SOS, about university studies, "In my life, no such opportunities have come at any time. Along the way, I had to find for myself and watch for opportunities, here and there for 'polishing my brains' from time to time. Thus I climbed slowly in a hit and miss way till I secured 10 university subjects and still lack five."

She had watched as the SOS had taken on a variety of innovative works that were only remotely associated with the original vision. In the original concept, missions were to be rural, focused on the needs of the developing frontier Church in the western provinces. She argued that priority should have been given to the small rural missions, projects that were now being overshadowed by the high-profile city hostels, catechetical centres and immigration work at Canadian ports. Biographer Jeanne Beck writes,

> Although the members now elected their Sister General and council, the order was still, in all essential matters, controlled by Father Daly. Because he had spent [the] order's money (which [Catherine] did admit he had worked very hard to raise) on

the urban properties used as hostels, very little would be available for the professional education of the sisters. This meant that the order would be ill-prepared to take advantage of the growing shortage of teachers and nurses. Catherine had met many of the novices at the correspondence schools in Regina and Edmonton, and she realized that during their training in Toronto they had never been told about her vision of women religious who would teach in the difficult rural areas. How could they understand the need for more training, if they were not told of the order's original purpose? The novices were only told that she was the first person to join the order.[29]

Although there were always efforts to establish rural missions in the western provinces, the Sisters of Service developed a variety of urban facilities, including those associated with their well-known correspondence courses for children. Historically, in spite of Catherine's efforts, the Sisters have been better remembered for these urban-based efforts than for the smaller rural public school missions that they conducted in the West. For example, in the pamphlet written by Philip J. Kennedy to celebrate the 100th anniversary of Catholic Missions in Canada in 2008, the Sisters of Service are acknowledged only for their catechetical correspondence course and their hostel work in the cities, although it is mentioned that the work aided immigrants and children in the West. This reflects how the Institute founded by Catherine Donnelly has come to be seen in the eyes of the Church and the Canadian public.[30]

The small, low-profile missions in isolated rural places, tiny seeds scattered far and wide in the open spaces of the West, never attained the public profile of the more visible urban missions, although the rural ones continued to form part of the overall SOS work. The high value Catherine placed upon these small rural outposts, and the fact that she was the founder of the SOS, is a matter of some significance, therefore. Her persevering struggle to turn the SOS's attention to these missions became a characteristic of her spirituality. Great energy, courage and endurance were required for her to stay faithful to her original inspiration. On the one hand, she resisted the paths taken by the community that seemed to contradict the original intentions of the founders. On the other, she laboured constructively to create models of working rural missions, and to convince others to do so as well – even if it meant going against the flow in their own community. Her spirituality communicates the qualities of both of these dispositions: resistance and cooperative action.

Eventually, Catherine began to express her unhappiness about the Institute's involvement in urban missions. She believed the city work to be behind the lack of attention that was being directed towards the rural teaching work in the West, arguing that the only reason a new Institute should come into being in the Church was to fulfill a new function. The rural missions were that new response of the Church – the response that no other Order was capable of making. Her sense of responsibility for the Institute eventually compelled her to launch a campaign to "tell the story" of the Institute's founding and true purpose.

As time passed and the Institute grew and developed, the community contemplated the necessity of recording the history of its founding and its ongoing development. Catherine began to speak of how Father Daly had come to be involved with the Institute, pointing out that the mission and charism of the community had already been established before his arrival. In 1968, she recalled the resistance she offered in those early days of the Institute:

> … attitudes could be completely mistaken about there not being dissent till later years. Dissent there was, constant and strong, and I was obliged to 'go underground' at times. Father Daley [sic] and some others began to show marked resentment to my ideas. I felt crushed and desperate. But I believed that Father Coughlan would still find some way of coming forward with authority and firmness as the great Cause for Nation, World and Church became in great danger of being ruined. And I well learned the guiding truth: 'To thine own self be true'. No other principle brings such peace of mind.

Although Father Coughlan could easily have cleared things up when questions began to surface about the founding of the community, he was unwilling to risk confronting Father Daly. In 1936, Coughlan had written to Catherine, expressing his reservations about putting together the true history of the founding of the Sisters of Service:

> I have not written a line of this history and I will now tell you what is holding me back. But this is a secret between you and myself, and I know you will keep it such. Father Daly is acknowledged everywhere as the founder of the Institute, and deservedly so from the standpoint of the valuable services he has rendered to it … Indeed I cannot see how the Institute could have continued its existence without him. But from a historical standpoint he is not the original founder. As far as I am concerned, I would be very glad to be left completely out of the picture. But if I am to write the history of the foundation of the S.O.S. I must tell the whole truth, and coming at this late date I am afraid that my account would annoy Father Daly and would give the impression that I wish to deprive him of the prestige of being the founder. The truth is, if you had not come to me with your story of Western conditions and your offer of yourself to make a beginning, there would be no S.O.S. today.

Father Coughlan never did write the history of the founding. After his death, it was left to Catherine to tell the story.

She began instructing others about how the Institute had deviated from the original vision. Her intention was to bring out the truth of the early history of the community, even though her story conflicted with the Sisters' own view of its beginnings. A core group listened to Catherine sympathetically and encouraged her to continue promoting a return to the original vision for the Sisters of Service. Catherine's early attempts to gain support for this effort received minimal attention within her community. As she ventured forth in the 1940s, the Catholic Church was still some time away from the renewal of religious life that would come about during Vatican II. She continued to hope that the rural mission model, which had proven successful, would convince the community to return to the vision of professionally trained religious women working in the harsh, remote regions of the West.

In 1940, when Catherine was 56 years old, she suddenly found herself in a place of deep personal crisis. Reflecting on this time in her life can help us to understand the reality of the burdens that contributed to her breakdown. It was a time during her spiritual journey when she experienced utter dependence upon God and other human beings for compassionate support, empathy and understanding. During her later years, her spirituality came to reflect the deep joy of having discovered her own worth as a woman of faith, as well as her discontent and restlessness as she pondered the obstacles and barriers to fully achieving her spiritual desires.

A series of events in Catherine's life marked a watershed in her activity towards educating the SOS about the early history of their Institute and the deviations from the original vision that had occurred under Father Daly's leadership. After overseeing the physically, mentally and emotionally exhausting project of establishing a school at Marquis, Saskatchewan, she had been sent immediately to begin what was known as a Continuation School at Sinnett, Saskatchewan. She arrived to discover that construction had hardly begun on the project. The Sisters were to live in the same building that housed the classroom, a building not yet divided into the appropriate sections, or adequately constructed to handle the harsh Saskatchewan winter. As the first day of school arrived, students and teacher were unable to use the building and headed outside to discuss the upcoming year. Catherine's concern, as always, was for her students. We can picture a middle-aged woman sitting on the grass with "thirteen quiet, courteous, eager" students, chatting about their future. Conversing with them, she learned that the girls wanted to become nurses. She immediately acted upon what she had learned, seeking out chemistry equipment so that the young women could follow their dreams.

Catherine had arrived at Sinnett full of optimism and enthusiasm for the new project. Besides extending the rural public school mission idea, this mission could perhaps revitalize the plan to use public schools as bases for the missionary activity of the Institute. She also saw this as a way to keep young people on their family farms, preventing the flow of youth to the cities in search of work. The Sinnett project was to be an opportunity for elementary school graduates to obtain their high school courses without having to leave their homes and travel to large cities.

When Catherine arrived in Sinnett, however, it was obvious something was wrong. A young and inexperienced Sister who had not yet made her final vows came to Sinnett with Catherine, but only as a homemaker for the mission. That left Catherine solely responsible for administration and teaching at the school. The other expected facets of her work – health care and social welfare work – were made nearly impossible due to a lack of time and the fact that the Sisters had no transportation. Even after the mission had been under way for some time, Sister Mary Quinn was prompted to comment on the terrible conditions of the place: "The place is a wreck ... I feel certain if you saw Sinnett you would not send a young inexperienced Sister there."

Deplorable conditions in the settlements were nothing new for Catherine. She had just come from Marquis where, as Father Coughlan pointed out, her experience "was enough to prostrate [her] in body and soul." None of the necessary preparations had been made at Sinnett either to house the Sisters or to teach the students. The parish priest and his housekeeper, along with the two Sisters, were the only people working to refit the building to accommodate the Sisters' quarters and the classroom. Catherine found herself not only teaching grades 9 through 11, but also overseeing more basic tasks like having students construct outhouses and a driving shed for their horses. The community had no electricity, and the Sisters struggled to keep snow out of the building as well as to keep the chimneys of their hand-me-down woodstoves from smoking and falling down. Simply hauling water was extraordinarily difficult. Distractions concerned Catherine as she was conscious that she must meet professional teaching requirements covering course standards set by the province.

Catherine was used to such hardships and would normally have carried on with her customary good nature and optimism. At other missions, however, she had received the help of the entire community in setting up the school. At Sinnett, she found nothing but chaos and apathy among the people, who left the religious to do everything associated with the mission. On an interpersonal level, this was distressing, but for Catherine it must have called the feasibility of her entire model of missionary work into question. Something was amiss in the relational dynamics of the community. No matter how hard she worked, she was not succeeding in generating the kind of transformation and enthusiasm that were known to be the fruits of the Sisters' efforts.

Catherine believed there were forces at work behind the scenes – secrets, deceptions and conditions that burdened her with more work than she could reasonably handle, subsequently leaving her little time for reflection. It appears that the pastor was complaining bitterly about Catherine to Sister General, while outwardly giving Catherine the impression that all was well. During class one day, she was handed a telegram from Toronto informing her that she was to leave the mission immediately, giving her no time to properly offer her resignation, to hand over responsibility to a successor or to learn the reason for her dismissal. The real reasons for what happened to Catherine in Sinnett remain shrouded in secrecy, but the situation left her contemplating this experience as an encounter with evil.

Catherine's sudden dismissal left her in a state of confusion and desolation. She described it in a letter to Sister General Agnes Dwyer in 1965:

> When the staggering blow came to me at Sinnett (what an outer-space adventure) I took it passively, utterly sick at heart, trampled in the dirt, completely friendless and despised apparently – but I sat quietly in the Lanigan hotel on a little chair in the corner of my bedroom and said to myself, "I will have Faith. This thing will pass away, and time will make me able to laugh at it.

Catherine regarded this as an experience of betrayal, not only towards herself, but also of the missionary work of the Sisters of Service. The affair affected her physically, mentally, emotionally and spiritually. It seemed she was intended to bear the brunt of the blame for the serious problems at the mission. Only hints and elusive comments that allude to these problems remain, along with the fact that the young and inexperienced Sister who came to Sinnett with Catherine returned to Toronto and left the Institute before making her final vows.

How did Catherine respond to this encounter with darkness, doubt and despair? For the first few days at Edson, where she was sent, she seems to have descended into depression. Edson was a bustling town located nearly 200 kilometres west of Edmonton, established as a local rail centre for the Canadian National Railway early in 1911. The busy St. John's Hospital cared for railway workers and their families, as well as farmers, miners and other workers from the surrounding areas. The Superior there, Sister Mary Quinn, SOS, gave Catherine the patient, loving care she needed. Sister Quinn watched over her and reported on her progress to Sister General. Her impression was that Catherine needed rest, and it seems she gently counselled Catherine when possible. Catherine always expressed gratitude for Sister Quinn's loving and wise ministrations. But, as she began to regain her strength, she recovered her resolve to return the focus of the SOS to the rural missions.

After Catherine's breakdown and recovery at Edson, she committed a great deal of time to consciously seeking vindication of the vision she had communicated to Father Coughlan and Archbishop McNeil during the founding days of the Institute. Her concerns reached far beyond merely gaining personal recognition for her part in establishing the SOS. Her indignation and anger caused her to speak out, more and more, about the conflict she had with Father Daly and those who embraced his vision for the SOS. To her, the original vision and the vision that had come to guide the Institute's activities were contradictory in many ways. She spoke more and more forcefully about the battle for power and control in the SOS.

In many ways, Catherine's spirituality resonated with the Book of Lamentations in the Bible, which is thought to be the work of witnesses to the destruction of Jerusalem, written in response to a horrific event in their history. Though the laments sound like funeral dirges, they also express hope and faith in God's steadfastness, because as Old Testament scholar Bernhard Anderson says, "in spite of the suffering that seemed to eclipse the sovereignty of God, these mourners stubbornly trusted in God's faithfulness."[31] Catherine's spirituality echoes this form of expression, revealing something about how she perceived her responsibility as the only person who knew the story of the founding of the SOS. At least part of this storytelling expressed her own mourning and grief over the death of her vision. Likewise, those truthful elements of Catherine's tale, which were most difficult to accept in the community, led to a surge of emotional response among the Sisters. Even though her desire was to correct errant understandings about the history of the Institute, Catherine's frustration, anger and despair finally found an outlet through her frequent communications.

As the details of the community's founding emerged and were verified, Catherine's significant role in the Institute's origins came to light. After seeking to know the truth of her experience, inspiration and involvement in the founding, the community formally acknowledged her as founder in 1990. The task of arriving at a clear knowledge of the history of the Institute from the time of its founding was taken even more seriously from that point, as the Sisters acquainted themselves with this key information.

·While Catherine did hold Father Daly responsible for taking the Institute off course, she never understood his errors to have compromised his holiness, his good intentions or his moral integrity. Instead, she believed it was his background and his commitment to the principles and values that had shaped his life that made it impossible for him to understand her ideas and plans. In an account of the SOS history written in the early 1970s, she commented:

> Father G. Daly, CSsR, had had no background in rural Western work, and definitely none in teaching in rural Western Public schools. With his typical Quebec and European home life, schooling and training he could not have the spirit of the true SOS Order which had been visualized and somewhat organized before he was sent for to come as a helper …

> That any man would attempt to grasp power to start a new community with a different purpose or mandate to the original and true SOS had never crossed my mind. But there were old forms; the old philosophy, the ideas about 'blind obedience' and the

'inferiority of women' in Quebec and elsewhere in those days. Women's rights and ecumenism had not become fashionable.

Catherine appears to have understood evil as an influential force resulting from unjust social conventions, customs and biases. Since God is the Creator, people are essentially good, but can be influenced towards evil. But, just as she acknowledged the reality of evil in her world, she also confessed her belief in the power of redemption. Her ways of understanding the power of evil, as well as her hope in redemption from evil, explain her long and painful struggle to confront any practice that prevented the original mission of the SOS from succeeding. Like St. Paul, she believed a force of evil was intentionally working in the systems of the human realm through a variety of influences. The influence of evil was personally involved in the world, working its will through deceptions, illusions and the natural human desire for power. Catherine attributed the problems she encountered in her relationship with Father Daly to cultural and intellectual developmental problems, saying he had been formed "by the school of thought which elevates the male human-being. Women were to listen, to leave leadership to men, even in ideas, an attitude now almost entirely gone from the intellectual world."

Catherine elevated the struggle taking place in the SOS, considering it in light of the cosmic struggle between good and evil that has occupied human beings from the time of creation. From a hopeful point of view, no part of creation could be considered to be beyond redemption, since all creatures carry within themselves the breath of life given to them by God. However, she perceived that evil could and did make use of the goods of creation for its own purposes. To this end, she often quoted Shakespeare in her letters: "The Devil can quote scripture for his purpose." With keen insight, she observed how certain ways of organizing society – based on deceptive and false ideals – led to imbalances of power and to injustice, promoting systems that profited some and burdened others. She frequently spoke of the blindness of those who were misled, even while she affirmed their essential goodness.

Even though Catherine acknowledged evil as a real threat to human development, she resisted dividing the world into safe places of goodness and dangerous places of evil. This certainly would never have satisfied her adventurous spirit or her constant search for God in all things. Something about being part of this quest on behalf of God's desire to transform the world energized her and gave her enthusiasm for life. Her zest for reform echoes Jesus' passionate exclamation: "I came to bring fire to the earth, and how I wish it were already kindled!" (Luke 12:49). This commitment to engagement with "the powers" meant Catherine had to deal with the reality of evil influences in a dynamic and ongoing way – as part of her everyday existence. Her faith orientation led her to believe that, with God's help, no evil would ultimately reign over the earth and its peoples. Her entrance into a religious community, therefore, did not release her from an obligation to struggle with the real problem of how evil operated in her world. Instead, she sought a community for support and camaraderie in the struggle.

Catherine did not conceive of the convent as a sacred place where evil could not enter. It would have been impossible for her and the other Sisters of Service to engage in social transformation in the way that they did if they had entertained such a notion. Catherine remained conscious of the influence of evil and the deep need of humans for conversion and transformation in all the contexts of her experience, including the SOS houses and the broader society.

Ultimately, Catherine came to believe that everything in her life was being transformed for the greater glory of God. In accepting this, she reflected with awe and appreciation for God's creative power on the mysterious path her life had taken. She acknowledged the limits of her own power, but placed great confidence in God's ability to transform even the worst situation – often paraphrasing a teaching from Ecclesiastes 7:13: "God writes straight with crooked lines." The quality and depth of her reflections changed as she moved through a number of life transitions – from a young woman into a mature middle-aged woman and, eventually, into old age. At the age of 84, she mused in a letter to Sister Patricia Burke,

'To thine own self be true' is a guide to me – and God is standing by. He has worked miracles. I came to Camp Morton under miserably heart-breaking restriction in 1924 knowing that I must endure every hardship, every scornful treatment by some of our own sisters and by the SOS officials whom I had brought into the project myself. Fr. A. Coughlan encouraged me to endure everything, to suffer willingly and to persevere.

Catherine relied upon her experiences to convince herself and others that there was still a way through life when all seemed bleak and hopeless. She remembered – and spoke of – her earlier experiences of weakness, exhaustion and breakdown, using language that revealed her feeling of being burdened, again writing to Sister Burke in 1978:

Today is the anniversary of my wonderful self-sacrificing Mother. She left us in 1905, 73 years ago. To me fell the responsibility of my two teenage sisters – aged 15 and 11. It was mountains of responsibility and I was crushed with worry about the influences they must be guided against. I had to be constantly alert for my own progress in teaching – needed the money – and always very keenly watching the circumstances connected with my two precious charges.

Soon came an almost complete breakdown for me – just too much physical, mental and emotional pressure and I barely escaped over the brink to 'no recovery' – six months of trying to think and plan again – and then another start at teaching and at keenly observing years of much variety of experience. I had to have the courage to dare and drive myself ahead in skill in teaching and getting along with people in general.

The words Catherine uses express her feelings of overwhelming burden – "mountains of responsibility," her feeling of being "crushed," her need to be "constantly alert." These are the words of one who senses she is all alone in the struggle. Attempts to gain control and maintain a semblance of mastery in a situation where she imagined herself to be floundering were simply too much to bear. In later life, especially in reaction to what she perceived to be Father Daly's resistance to listening to her ideas, Catherine used the same kind of language to describe her sense of burden. For example, in describing the resistance she experienced in the community, she wrote, "I felt crushed and desperate."

At several points in her life, Catherine seemed caught between trusting in her own capability and competency and dealing with her feelings of inadequacy and powerlessness. Although she planned and fretted about the missions, her spirit drove her to seek God and to attribute tremendous power to prayer – prayer, that is, intended to support action. A spiritual guide whom she admired and trusted, Father Coughlan, influenced her by counselling her to work hard and to trust God to redeem human activity.

Before heading out west, Catherine made her way through the rural school system of Ontario seeking higher-paying positions, grateful that her professional qualifications made it possible for her to support and care for her family. As she explained later, "Schools offering the highest salaries had to be hunted out by me and handled successfully. It was a must!" Her success in meeting these demands was bittersweet. She necessarily lived where her work took her, leaving her father alone. Later in life, she regretted this distance, noting that her father suffered terrible loneliness, anxiety and depression after the death of his wife and the loss of his farm. Catherine later chided herself for not realizing how much he needed her, writing to her cousin Betty Ogle: "I think I did not manage resourcefully enough to give my lonely father … company and care and attention enough." Her own suffering sharpened her awareness of the need to be present to others.

Although she regretted her mistakes, weaknesses and failures, she did not allow her memories of them to drive her into unhealthy guilt or self-recrimination. Full of hope, and trusting in God, she spoke of her excitement about meeting her family members in heaven. In fact, she reflected that her feelings about heaven were something like her experience of homesickness when she was a young woman. In a letter to Sisters Patricia Burke and Anna McNally in 1979, she expressed it like this:

I look back now at that time when I left our farm house briefly and got very horribly home-sick. What pure joy when my dear Father came for me and I was briefly with my dear, dear family again. I want to be with him [Hugh Donnelly] and my wonderful mother and their other children in Heaven – am home-sick again. And this old planet does seem to be in a whirl of troubles, doesn't it?

In stories of spiritual transformation there is always evidence of a change of heart. Catherine, a burdened and striving young woman, allowed her trust in God's providence to bring her to the point where she could offer herself completely as a servant to the poor of the West. At each transition in her life, she let go of certain things of the past so she could enter into a new phase of activity and understanding. Catherine's faith in God's providence helped her recognize that there were limits to her power. This did not make her exempt from pursuing goals, dreams and desires, but she saw her own activities as taking place within a greater economy of salvation. Expressing this view in her praise of the spirituality of Sister Renaud, she exclaimed in a letter to a friend in 1980,

> When we see and hear and think and have a will to do what is needed, there is action straight ahead – do our very best and God will do the rest [...] Sr. L. Renaud is an example of deep true Christianity in action. SOS needs hundreds of such – practical facing of reality – knowing reality by grasping it and expecting no reward of any special type except – that of Eternity. [...] 'Life is short – eternity is forever' is what she keeps in mind. Her talents are countless and willingly used.

Catherine's practical and down-to-earth spirit kept her shoulder to shoulder with the people she served. Her trust in God's transforming power expanded her hope in the future. She handled challenges with a sense of optimism and a sense of humour that walked hand in hand with the way of compassion. This deep faith infused her human relationships with energy. She viewed human suffering against the horizon of hope in ultimate redemption. The following spiritual advice, offered to a young Sister, speaks of the intense energy Catherine believed came from her deep desire to know God in the world, along with her deep faith that God heard and answered her prayers. As she told Sister Adua Zampese, SOS, in a letter in 1975,

> The wisest thing to do is find out reality in all the phases of your life there – and then face right up to the 'reality' head-on, with all your talents and potential – and leave the rest to God! Keep to prayer – prayer with Faith. Be quite sure that God is listening and Faith in Him is what pleases Him greatly – the time, the place, the situation you are in, do not matter – just your need and your absolute Faith! Truly.

Father Coughlan sensed Catherine's struggles to find some spiritual equilibrium between her tremendous drive and her need to seek comfort and rest in God. Even Catherine knew herself to be "a restless little scamp at times." Father Coughlan seemed to think her single-mindedness of purpose and high energy were somewhat masculine qualities, leaving her lacking in qualities normally associated with feminine and maternal roles of women religious. He commented to Sister Florence Regan, Sister General in 1936, "I know her well, and she is really a woman of faith and high purposes, and her energy is unbounded. If she had more of the mother in her make-up, and a better grasp of spiritual values, what a flower she would be in your Institute!" He noted Catherine's tendency to shoulder too much of the weight of hardship and struggle in the community projects she undertook, but acknowledged the courage, the love and the profound devotion to God that were expressed in her spirituality. He clearly believed that her whole life had been transformed in service of God and neighbour:

> I cannot help but admire the courage with which you have met trying conditions not only during your religious career but also before you became a Sister of Service. Some of these earlier trials I know. They have all made you able to understand people and places, to see clearly the needs, especially of the West, and to devote yourself intelligently and zealously to remedy these needs.

Always restless, always seeking to promote her vision of rural missionary work, Catherine was challenged to accept the limits of her personal power and to let God take care of the rest. Like Julian of Norwich and others whose image of God focused on divine providence, Catherine came to understand that all would be well. Instead of excusing her from the arduous work of questing for the reign of God on earth, however, this hope spurred her onward: "It is not glaring success which counts – but endeavour. My endeavour started in 1918 and is a long and twisted road. But 'God writes straight with crooked lines.'"

It may seem that Catherine's outbursts were all directed towards other people, especially towards Father George Daly, who organized and led the SOS for so many years. A closer look reveals much more about her inner turmoil, however. Jeanne Beck notes that "Catherine never ceased to blame herself for agreeing to have Father Daly appointed to help organize and direct the Institute in its early stages."[32] Catherine's letters reveal the force and emotion behind her words when she spoke of her fault. Although there were many statements of forgiveness for others, it is uncertain whether she consciously sought forgiveness for her own failure. The only indication of her finding forgiveness, peace and consolation is her constant insistence that God would somehow straighten out whatever deviations had occurred and make everything right in the end.

Her need to persuade the community to listen to her caused her to agitate and urge others to action. She believed that weak commitment to the original charism of the Institute had made it possible for the entire community to become distracted from its call – a call towards which she felt personally responsible. The spiritual energies supplied by God, along with the inspiration and the resources for the mission of the SOS, were therefore being dispersed, making the Institute ineffective in achieving its aims. As she often pointed out, the need was still present in the context in which the original call had been received.

In letter after letter, Catherine wrote to the Sisters complaining about the innovations that were added to the original vision. Her passionate desire for a return to this focus in the work of the SOS had some adverse side effects. In later years, as she helped others with the upgrading of their education, she drove them with such determination that they often found it difficult to endure her loud speaking voice and the rigorous demands of her lessons. Other Sisters were sometimes hurt by her insensitive comments about the different types of work they did in the Institute's missions.

Catherine's angst grew as she considered the declining power of her vision within the Institute. From the rural settlements, she had envisioned that the Sisters would reach beyond their boundaries to seek out the most isolated and abandoned people. This outreach would continually draw the Sisters towards the margins of society, where there were people who needed all forms of assistance. The direction of the Institute's progress would, therefore, be away from the centralized, urban centres. In the early Rules and Constitutions, the work of the Institute is described in the following way:

> Since the life of the Sisters of Service is one consecrated to the apostolate of Catholics most destitute of spiritual help, particularly among the immigrants and their children dwelling in the outlying districts, they should always have before their eyes the specific work for which they were founded.

Catherine had enthused that the work would be rural, and that it would not seek to imitate the work of the older orders but would complement their work. In that way, she thought, an attitude of respect for those older traditions could be generated in the new community. Necessary reforms could go forward as responses to requirements in new fields of missionary work. She believed this was the only reason for beginning any new Institute in the Church. In her experience, the older orders were *unable* to respond to the needs of the people in this new field, a circumstance that legitimated the establishing of an entirely new religious community.

Catherine was sensitive to the struggles of all who were poor. She was keenly interested in developing programs whereby these people would be embraced by Canadians and become Canadians who would then embrace others. Her concern was for their sense of belonging, well-being and development, just as she was concerned with the sense of belonging, well-being and development of the women in her Institute. This may seem to contradict the selflessness required of religious women at that time, but Catherine had a vision for women that sought meaningful work for them, happiness and fulfilment in their civic life, and full and rich benefits of belonging in a religious community with cooperating coworkers.

Some of Catherine's frustration arose because she was genuinely concerned about the happiness of the women who worked in the SOS. Her vision for all SOS women was inspired by her own sense of daring and adventure. She was convinced that the *inspirational* aspect of the Institute's foundations had to do with crossing over existing boundaries in the Church's mission, taking brave steps into new territories and being willing to let go of old customs when necessary. Another reason for her stubbornness in insisting on the community's return to its original mission was her own struggle within the dynamics of power that are always at work in the institutions of the Church. For Catherine, this was particularly true of the struggle to recognize the equality of women and their right to work side by side with men in the mission of Christ. She desired to be heard as a person of vision.

Catherine admitted that she enjoyed being something of a crusader for the rights of the downtrodden. This motivation fuelled at least part of her battle for recognition of the original vision for the Sisters of Service, as well as her criticism of the innovations and new ventures that she believed had distracted the community and depleted essential resources. She thought that she and Father Coughlan had enjoyed a partnership of equals, and there is a great deal of evidence in their letters to support this. But Father Coughlan had also advised Catherine to resist taking on a leadership role in the Institute, and he backed away from challenging Father Daly's authority with regard to the Institute. While it is clear that Father Coughlan eagerly sought Catherine's advice on most details of the new Institute before he handed its care to Father Daly, her influence was minimal after that point. Since there were few formal ways to express her anger, confusion and disappointment, these often erupted in bombastic comments in her letters and conversations.

Catherine learned in later years, from Father Daly himself, that he had not understood the way that the public school system worked in the western provinces, and therefore could not fully appreciate the innovative missionary model proposed at the beginning of the Institute. The truth is that the central ideas of the original mission *did* survive and continued to develop within the Institute's overall missionary program. The rural mission was not abandoned, although focus on innovative projects prevented its more vibrant growth. Some of the novices who entered and were suitable for the work became teachers and nurses and social welfare workers in the rural areas of the mission field. These women continued in the tradition of Catherine Donnelly's vision for the rural West, giving her hope that the original vision was being preserved within the Institute.

Catherine's suffering, the grace that she encountered, and the transformation she underwent in her own conversion each contributed to her ongoing relationship with God. She sought God's help in the presence of the Holy Spirit, and she believed divine truth was revealed in the person of Jesus Christ. She embraced her experience of divine mystery and responded to its lure towards deeper and fuller humanity. Catherine's journey, step by courageous step, led her towards human fullness. In her later years, by all accounts, she mellowed and was more at peace. She spent a great deal of time in prayer, keeping her rosary close, wearing it around her neck. She comfortably confessed to many Sisters that she wished she could have found more time for prayer, a sure sign that she came to appreciate its power even more in her last years.

Throughout her long life, Catherine believed that prayer was good for *her* – not that it was necessary for God. She considered spiritual fidelity to prayer, work and worship to be a personal responsibility. In her writings she spoke of Heaven as a place where all humans would fully understand the simple message of Jesus' prayer to the Father. It would be a place where all relationships were reconciled, a vision that calmed Catherine's unsettled mind and soothed her conscience. As she wrote to Sister Patricia Burke in 1979,

God has allowed a great deal of misunderstanding, of obstruction, of bungling, because of human weakness. We cannot blame any one certain thing or person – and I feel that those who were in contact and interested in any way and have left this world – have Light which shone not for their eyes when on earth. There had [been] big personal problems – sometimes the surprises I got were utterly stunning for me and I failed somewhat perhaps by being inclined to resent and let a kind of untrusting attitude take over.

The Lord's prayer is perfect "Forgive us our trespasses as we forgive."

When Catherine reflected on the meaning and value of the Lord's Prayer in her spiritual life, she did not focus on what it asked of God, but rather what it asked of her. She did not allow its spiritual meaning to be divorced from its moral meaning, but allowed the prayer to inform her moral life with wisdom. Prayer, then, in Catherine's understanding, was a support for those who worked towards the realization of God's will in the world – a way of constantly orienting themselves towards the unfolding reign of God in real, concrete ways. In an open letter to all the Sisters of Service in 1968, she wrote, "Prayer must fortify work. It must be earnest prayer – not necessarily long drawn out prayers. A short prayer by a thief on a cross did marvels. Prayer must not be such as to obstruct necessary works of charity."

Catherine believed prayer helps people appreciate the wonder and mystery of God's creative power as evidenced in the world all around us, even though the imperfection of our lives might suggest otherwise. It might be said that her prayer was hope. She looked to nature and its creatures to fuel her trust in God. Her favourite prayer, she said, was "The Prayer of St. Francis" – a prayer that taught her to appreciate the gentleness and peacefulness she encountered in her relationships with other creatures. According to all who knew her, Catherine's prayer life remained grounded in her love of nature, of creatures and of human beings, especially those most in need. Her encounter with God in prayer was an ongoing conversation as she encountered the divine in her world.

Catherine prayed for courage, as well as for protection from the dangers of religious adventure. She sought healing for her suffering, and the patience to accept her failures. In a submission to the SOS in 1974, Catherine included the following poem:

> *He who has dared, has done*
> *Whether he lost or won.*
> *No man has failed, who tried*
> *Whether he lived or died.*
>
> *This is the truest Truth*
> *Age would impart to youth*
> *Only a few prevail*
> *But only the quitters fail.*
>
> *Christ on a bloody cross*
> *Yet who can call it loss?*
> *One He had thought his friend*
> *Whispered, "It is the end!"*
>
> *But where in the cruel crowd*
> *Where are the princes proud?*
> *Dead like the mists of dawn*
> *Only the Christ lives on.*
>
> *Honour is not alone*
> *Laurel or wreath or throne*
> *Many a heart as brave*
> *Sleeps in a loser's grave.* [33]

In her adventurous life, Catherine acknowledged that her daring choices could only be validated by waiting for the fruits of action to appear. Since human societies are often slow in evolving, she knew it was reasonable to expect to wait a long time for validation. She reflected on the fact that trust is tested in life, but that faith requires deep trust and willingness to look beyond the obstacles. She noted that often those conventional methods and practices in which humans put so much faith seemed to be obstacles that prevented progress. She had confronted customs that had come to be accepted without question, and she had advocated for a new intelligence. She relied upon imagination to seek out novel pathways into the future, recognizing that this required willingness to risk. Her community consciousness led her to insist on freedom within the institution to creatively search for new methods and techniques.

Catherine's hope was grounded in both this world and the next. She believed that if people were courageous, together they could overcome obstacles and find fuller, better humanity. Creation's future was a good future because it moved towards complete reconciliation in the unity of God. She placed her hope not in ideas about God or humans, but in the fundamental goodness of people and in her genuine encounters with God's grace. She could be stubborn and tenacious, but she was also a person who could let go. She willingly walked with people and then trusted them – and God – to carry on the work. This attitude graced her with an outlook that focused on what was working, and her positive descriptions filled her letters to others. She knew the power of transformation was within the people she served, as evidenced in one of her letters to Sister Avila, CSJ, in 1974:

> The wise and humble boys and girls of the first days of Loyola Continuation School founded an institution of which we may all be proud today. Without their loyal spirit it could never have been done. May the generations to come follow, always, this tradition! With God all things are possible!

Perhaps nothing illustrates Catherine Donnelly's pragmatic, unadorned spirituality better than this short prayer written at the end of a note: "May God help each of us to look with Hope to the Future."

Sister Catherine took obstacles in stride, as shown by her practical approach
to this tree that lay in her path during the catechetical tour in the Cariboo.

❧ Chapter Nine ❧

The Spiritual Legacy of Catherine Donnelly

Catherine Donnelly's message to her Sisters and to the Church was, "Launch out into the deep. Don't hold back because there are risks. If there is a work to be done, obstacles must be demolished. God will provide the means if we but seek them." This was the life Catherine Donnelly lived. This is her legacy to the Church.

Father Grant Jahnke, OMI

The grounds of the Ignatius Jesuit Centre in Guelph, Ontario, are home to the Catherine Donnelly Walk. Appropriately, the path meanders between ploughed fields on the one side and a meditative walk called "The Stations of the Cosmos" on the other. Stately conifers, several metres high, line the short walk, making it a sheltered and defined "place in between." Stepping onto the path, one can contemplate the tilled landscape reminiscent of the hard work of farming the land and, turning, appreciate the tremendous wonder of the great gift of creation. The path, dedicated to Catherine, reflects her reverence for creation, her love of nature and agriculture, and her concern that people live organic, personal and spiritual lives. This speaks of an ecological spirituality – a spirituality attuned to the rhythms of nature and the cosmos.

The Catherine Donnelly Walk acknowledges the way her spirituality resonated with Jesuit spirituality and is a tribute to her holistic approach to life and mission. Catherine drew spiritual strength and inspiration from many sources in the Church – certainly from the Redemptorist mission of seeking out those most in need, and also from the Jesuit practice of seeking God in all things. As well, the Sisters of Service (SOS) and the Society of Jesus (Jesuits) are both communities dedicated to the development of a spirituality that reverences creation, fosters ecological awareness and is especially attentive to protecting environments that are threatened through neglect and abuse.

Like so many great innovators, Sister Catherine Donnelly beckoned others to follow her along new pathways of discovery and learning. She left a rich and unique spiritual legacy. In addition to her gift of a holistic vision and the integrity of her life, her many other gifts have been acknowledged by those who have learned about her life. The Catherine Donnelly Foundation offers tribute to her religious and social contributions: "Blessed with a profound understanding of people's spiritual, social and cultural needs, she conceived and implemented new ways of being church where the church was not present."[34]

Why does her spirituality matter today? Her own hope would be for us to reflect upon our need for "common sense" – a favourite term of Catherine's – as we consider our future together as Canadians. The term "common" implies that we share things, beginning with environments in which we live. It also implies that we explore, through dialogue, the meanings, values and beliefs that offer possibilities for unity. She would suggest we discover the Catholic Church's role in Canadian society by identifying the real needs of all Canadians, and then by reflecting together on possible responses to those needs. In forming our responses, she would expect us to ask practical questions of our theology – to question the real and concrete difference our theology makes in the world in which we live.

She would expect us to dare in ministry – looking beyond the identified margins to small isolated pockets of the poor and the needy. In other words, she would expect us to be as restless as she was in her search for justice for *all* of God's creatures. She would likely have much to say about the quality and nature of religious life for women, and would proudly note the continuing influence of women on Canadian social development.

Emerging from within a tradition of Christian women who have lived prophetically, often publicly calling the Church's attention to its own need for institutional reform, Catherine's spiritual legacy consists in so much more than her courageous questioning of institutional practices. Its value continues as she invites us to examine our notions of community development, of the Church's relation to the world in which it lives, and the importance of the experience of *encounter* in Christian ministry and missionary work. She invites us to be newly inspired by the story of creation and to find gratitude in our hearts for the gift of nature. She reintroduces us to those strong biblical themes that speak of the human quest for liberation and salvation. She asks us to situate ourselves realistically within a world that is both blessed and broken, experiencing solidarity with one another in genuine friendship that calls every one of us to both accountability and forgiveness.

Catherine was willing to question authority when its dictates contradicted her own sense of mission. She leaves us with questions about how to understand the nature of authority and obedience in the Church today. She was adamant she could not be a puppet. Theologian Sandra Schneiders helps us to better understand Catherine's disposition:

> ... the prophet is not a puppet. Everything depends on the prophet's obedience, the prophet's 'yes.' Jesus' 'Be gone, Satan' and choice to serve God alone (Mt. 4:10) in response to God's choice of him as 'Beloved Son' or Mary's 'Be it done to me according to [God's] word' (Lk. 1:36) in response to her call to be the mother of the messiah, exemplify the partnership of God and the prophets in the great work to which God calls them.[35]

Catherine's willingness to obey the call from God from the time when she first became conscious of it in 1918 is a testimony to us. Her story of risk taking and religious adventure causes us to reflect on the spiritual significance of her life. If she had simply followed the directions of her superiors in the Institute without question, she would likely never have come to our attention at all.

Novelty and tradition were both present in Catherine's response as she established a new way for the Church to respond to the needs of souls. She drew upon Scripture, Christian tradition and the broader human history of the rise and fall of civilizations. She interpreted the meaning of past events, teachings, doctrines and cultures to respond to the questions of her time. Interpretation has been part of the Church's tradition since its beginning. From the time of the inauguration of the Christian community, interpreting the prophetic call of the Gospel in the midst of current crisis was the hermeneutical activity that kept the community of Jesus' followers from despairing.[36] Catherine followed in the footsteps of those who dared interpret the meaning and value of the Gospel for their own times and places.

Catherine disposed herself towards the Christian mission by allowing *need* to become the fundamental driving principle of her Christian action. Her rich religious heritage offered basic wisdom – a treasury of teachings to help her in identifying the true needs present in any human situation. At its heart was this statement of Jesus: "I was hungry and you gave me food; I was thirsty and you gave me something to drink; I was a stranger and you welcomed me; I was naked and you gave me clothing; I was sick and you took care of me; I was in prison and you visited me" (Mt. 25:35-36). Hunger, thirst, alienation, extreme poverty, illness and the breakdown of compassionate societies – all of these conditions lead to loss of dignity among God's people. These are conditions that threaten to destroy communities. A host of Catholic saints and founders of religious communities have made it their mission to seek out and help the poor. For example, Catherine and all the Sisters of Service were visibly influenced by the spirituality of St. Alphonsus, who, living among the shepherd people of Scala, Italy, discovered that their need for God's love inspired him. With deep trust that God would provide for their own basic needs, they turned their attention outward to extend the reach of God's love to those who most needed to encounter it. Catherine, committed to a full and rich vision of education in rural communities, practised a form of discernment that kept her seeking for those most in need. At the same time, she discovered grace as the presence of God was revealed in her students and their families. Their need was, for her, the fermenting ingredient that extended the reign of God by inviting her to step beyond what was formerly possible in order to embrace new life in Christ.

Catherine repeatedly exclaimed, "Nothing is impossible with God!" Her interpretation of the Gospel mission therefore placed its priority upon what was already present in the context – the need of the other. Her missionary ingenuity called upon her to discern within the given context what resources God was making available as a response to the needs of people. This practical discernment consistently kept Catherine from allowing institutional deficiencies to defeat her in proposing responses. In order to accept such a freeing power in ministry, she depended upon deep faith in God's providence.

One of the predominant themes in Catherine's interpretation of Scripture and Christian tradition was the self-sacrificing nature of the Church as a body. She truly believed that the Church follows Christ. Therefore, the Church *always* exists for the sake of the world, and not primarily for its own sake. Catherine was decisive in her choice to follow a religious path that centred her attention on the needs of others – especially those most at risk spiritually. This was, for her, the path of personal religious perfection. She interpreted Christ's teaching to mean that she must allow the needs of the poorest of the poor to evoke her compassion, love and desire for justice in genuine Christian service. This is a radical interpretation, and one that causes us to reflect on the Church's own constant need for deeper trust in God's providence.

Part of the Church's tradition has been ongoing analysis of the effectiveness of religious institutions in serving the needs of people. As a result, some aspects of institutional life are found to be outdated and obsolete. Catherine questioned the need to remain loyal to outmoded institutional norms for women religious if these norms got in the way of serving the people of God. Her freedom made it possible for her to lead the Church into new ways of ordering its activities. This type of reform was not new in the Church's tradition, but her actions mean she takes her place in a long tradition of prophecy and prophetic action within the Church's history. Her authenticity, as she responded to her unique call, was the reason why *The Catholic Register*, in 2000, included her name in its list of the top ten Catholics whose influence shaped the Church in Canada. She truly did persuade the Church to risk allowing the Holy Spirit to lead Canadian Catholics forward into something new.

As Catherine reflected on appropriate activity in religious life for SOS members, she focused on discernment of need and feasibility. In doing so, she invites us to consider how the Church's institutions can better serve human beings in the reality of their needs today. In her time, she witnessed that social and cultural developments were making it possible for women to offer themselves as human resources for the good of Church and society. This required confronting institutional practices that excluded women from service for reasons rooted in bias, discrimination and prejudice. She saw that, in the Church, women were forced into roles that limited the ways they could offer themselves, so she set out to change this – beginning with her own life.

The identity of women within the Church of Catherine's time was understood largely in terms of the limits placed upon their social roles. Institutional custom in traditional orders imposed strict rules on Catholic women religious. Systematic theologian Margaret Lavin points out that today, our relationship to institutions must be approached with maturity. We must critically examine the ways in which we allow institutions to determine our identity. Her words capture Catherine's own spirit of reform in addressing the Church of her time: "The key issue is that we understand ourselves as freely, and interdependently, working *within* [institutions], not defined by them. We are God's, and it is God who defines who and what we are."[37]

As a devout listener for God's Word in Scripture, Catherine remained attuned to a life lived in community, encountering God's presence as a *personal* reality. In her time, the *vertical* relationship of people with God could sometimes become detached from the *horizontal* relationship of people within the web of human community. As this happened, many believed it possible to develop a relationship with God, but experienced no equal desire to develop their relationship with neighbours. Religious practice became a private matter between God and the individual, compromising the integrity of the command to love *both* God and neighbour. Love of both God *and* neighbour mean Christian love can never be removed from its practical expression in public. The object of Catherine's devotion, therefore, never became an abstraction: the religious and moral dimensions of her faith were woven together so that God's Word to her always commanded a moral response.

A Church focused on others is capable of testifying to the spiritual gifts of those who are not part of our identified community. For this reason, Catherine rejoiced when she witnessed the compassion of others, regardless of their religious denomination or tradition. She was able to acknowledge the organic and personal networks of relationship that together fostered the growth of true community. To her, creation was truly *one body*, and she was concerned with the health of that body. This is wisdom for us as we realize the threats confronting the personal dimensions of our societies, as well as those challenging the organic base of the ecological systems that sustain us.

As a founder, Catherine's genius was that she perceived that early intervention in the development of societies could influence growth in compassion, responsibility, mercy, justice, peace and unity, especially in those societies where all members were severely affected by poverty and injustice. The organization of a Christian community, she believed, must serve to remind us that God's personal relationship with creation is the source of people's power to grow and become. Because she experienced the growth of community as natural and personal, she humbly and gratefully looked beyond her own power to the source of each community's life – God's spirit alive in nature and among the people. This disposition constituted an ongoing act of worship in her life. With this appreciation came deep humility and gratitude for what God was making possible among the people of the West.

Catherine was aware of the Church's need for ongoing critique of culturally and religiously rooted bias, and believed that such critique must become part of the Church's reforms. For example, while "human" is the most basic category for our species, male and female are secondary distinctions that need not limit the possibility of equality and mutuality within the Church. Catholic, Protestant, Jewish, Hindu, Buddhist, Muslim – these, likewise, are further distinctions that need not limit the possibility of equality and mutuality in society. Gender discrimination is one form of bias that continues to plague the Church. Religious discrimination is another. Our motivation for remedying all discriminatory practices lies in acknowledging our need for one another. Ecumenical and interfaith movements remain ineffective so long as the Catholic Church's members consider themselves entitled to acknowledge the permanency of barriers to dialogue. In our recent history, the Church's leadership has been called upon to be more open to conversation about gender equality, ecumenical unity and the adoption of a more appreciative stance towards other religions. Catherine's experience as a pioneer within the Canadian Catholic Church's development illustrates the need for such a dialogical approach to the question of equality in opportunities for ministry and leadership within the Church. There is much to be learned from Catherine and her life.

Catherine discovered that social and political developments in the western provinces made something possible in the SOS's ministry that remained impossible for other orders. Women of faith found a place in the professions that served a developing society, and then invited the Church to learn what God was making possible in the world. In Canadian society, women were moving into public roles as professionals, as thinkers, speakers and writers, as citizens concerned with questions of justice and responsibility. Catherine realized that this development offered an opening for the Church to structure itself in new ways to meet the needs of all people in a frontier environment, and she believed that women had an important part to play in this development.

Canadian Nellie McClung noted that women brought a new imagination to bear upon present concerns, and their daring actions were reshaping the world. She wrote, "Woman's place in the new order is to bring imagination to work on life's problems. Without vision, which is another word for imagination, the people perish."[38] As Catherine slowed down the pace of her active life in the peaceful environment of Camp Morton, she insisted her imagination was still a vital part of her intelligence: "My imagination was working in the right direction 50 years ago and I feel convinced that it is still OK. I cook and bake and clean floors and go on imagining; I write letters and do a bit of gardening – and keep on imagining."

It was Catherine's active imagination that led her to seek wholeness in her life, integrating faith and responsibility to help shape the society in which she lived. She wanted everyone, especially women, to be aware of opportunities present in the culture – opportunities that she understood to be calling the Church to new life. She was not naive, however, and knew that change would challenge both men and women, especially those who found their security and identity in the religious structures and roles as they existed.

Catherine confronted the systems of entitlement she had encountered within the Church – patriarchal systems that viewed women as inferior to men, or as less capable for ministry and missionary work. She also confronted those systems that promoted the belief that Catholics were superior to those of other faith systems. She supported Church leaders who tried to heal the harm done to women who suffered because of the prevalence of such influences. In a letter to Sister Mary Reansbury in 1967, she stressed,

> It might just be a catastrophe if any of us follow the old foolish and false idea that men are superior to women – that we cannot think for ourselves. Surely we are real people, real women. And Cardinal Suenens is only one of the thousands of wise theologians who scorn the decadent idea and teaching that women are inferior to men and must have men for guidance in the policy of their Institutes.

Catherine challenged systems of entitlement that, for many Canadians, seemed unquestionably entrenched in the sacred structures of the Church, or in its theology. That is, she challenged the notion that men held superior power within the Church because God *wanted it that way*. Her spirituality suggested a direction of humility for all members, and not just the raising of women's status in the Church. In living this out, she put her faith to work in concrete situations of need. She argued that the needs of others required women to step over barriers to inequality. She believed responsible women should go ahead in assuming and acting upon their equal place in the mission of the Church and pointed to her own actions to illustrate what was necessary: "It was most painful to be expected to be a mere puppet. That did not work with me – ever. And I had to pay the price of insisting on being a 'person.'"

What does Catherine's spirituality suggest as the way of reform? Her life and her actions teach us it will be *need* that ignites the desire for unity and equality in the Church's life. Catholic Christianity is rooted in our knowledge of our need – for God and for one another. The contributions of every member of the Body of Christ on earth helps advance the mission of the Church. Each person in the missions, therefore, was a needed and valued member of the Church for Catherine and she would not rest until they knew it!

Catherine's integral spirituality reminds us that all creation is whole and holy, and overflowing with value that ultimately can be discovered only through encounter with the divine presence hidden in all things. Mysteriously, though, evil is also part of our experience, and our tradition tells us it always has been. Scripture tells us that the serpent was present in the Garden of Eden before humans responded to its enticements to take and act against what God desired for them. It seems that, from the very beginning of creation, God has required that we be willing to choose between or among the paths that lie at our feet. As Catherine reflected on this point, she came to understand that a God-given capacity for judgment and decision was given to us to be used and developed in our everyday lives – including in matters concerned with religion.

As an adult, Catherine knew herself to be a responsible evaluator and decision maker, capable of both good and evil. She approached her life, mission and ministry as one who bent an ear to the ground to *listen* to what was happening around her. She interpreted the words of Scripture in ways that helped her to choose what she called "the right track," often finding startling new ways of understanding the text in light of her own problems and concerns. She turned to prayer to help her choose God's way, and to help her resist what led her away from God's desire for her. She depended upon a rich tradition of scriptural wisdom, Church teaching, philosophy, art, science and history to guide her understanding of the choices that lay before her. As she noted, "Religion as an isolated subject is taken out of context." She was willing to take chances, and to entertain the possibility of choosing wrongly. She did not see inactivity or passivity as an option in the Christian life, although she learned to surrender her will when it became obvious her goal was not immediately possible. She saw the world as a dynamic reality that was constantly moving towards the future, and change as part of that reality.

Change made it necessary – and often forced Catherine – to make difficult choices, and she believed in her own accountability. She learned she could either allow others to shape her life through their judgments and decisions or she could become an intelligent and responsible actor. Catholic tradition considers human beings as "artisans of our own destiny," an expression Pope Paul VI used in the encyclical *Populorum Progressio*. Catherine embodied this beautiful image in many ways. The responsibility of the individual – to know, to judge and to decide for himself or herself – has perhaps never been more urgently needed than it is in our current time. Our institutions, doctrines and dogmas can help us in our tasks, but they cannot ultimately *choose* or *prefer* one path or another. Only people can decide how they will dispose themselves responsibly towards their own present circumstances and towards their shared future. Governments will not save the environment, for example, by legislating responsibility unless willing citizens acknowledge a shared responsibility for the stewardship of their environment and agree to walk in the way of that path.

Catherine's spiritual inclinations, as interpreted in this account of her spirituality, lead us to consider what she invites us to as responsible agents within God's saving mission. Her focus on the inspiration of personal encounter in conjunction with her deep love of natural environments speaks of a theology that communicates our *need* for the natural world, as well as our *need* for one another. Her desire for equality and liberation invoke the dismantling of systems of entitlement that seek to justify attitudes of superiority or inferiority as a basis for social development. Thus, both within the Church's structures and in the broader society, Christians will seek to uncover and heal the root causes of social division, aiming to liberate both those who mistakenly co-opt the areas of responsibility rightfully belonging to others and those who powerlessly endure restrictions to living fully responsible lives.

Consistently, Catherine hoped for reform in the systems of thought that have, over centuries, taken on authoritative value in the life of the Church, clearly linking thought and behaviour. Her strong emphasis on need and feasibility remind us that, since Jesus made the need of the other a determining factor in the activity of his followers, the Church is *primarily* pastoral. Thinking about God is part of the ongoing process of theological reflection, but the Church's mission was born of Jesus' loving and compassionate actions. Christ's mission highlights the place of *encounter* in the lives of Christians. This confronts an understanding of the Church's mission as one of conveying truth to others in terms of facts and ideas.

A vibrant human being on a quest for the truth about what God wants for all people, Catherine knew she was not perfect, but she did think of herself as courageous. Because she allowed faith to lead her into adventure, she encountered hazards and dangers. She slipped and fell, but then got up again to go forward. Her spirituality offers a wonderful illustration of how humans navigate the spiritual life. She proposed an ecclesiology of *friendship*, the kind of friendship that called others to account for their humanity and urged them to fully participate in the personal life they shared with one another.

Catherine's spirituality also invites us to learn more about her concern for the agricultural way of life and its significance for our spirituality. Indeed, farming was more than a way of life for her; it was an orientation towards creation and the place of human work in that creation. Many of her values were formed in light of her concern for the health of the land as a nourishing place for earth's inhabitants. Today, in the work of agrarian philosophers and ecologists, we hear echoes of her anxiety about the dangers facing farmers and rural residents. Beyond our urgent ecological problems, there are serious concerns that we are losing touch with our agrarian heritage. This heritage will be lost if we abandon practices of responsible stewardship towards our places in the world. Spiritually, we are faced with the prospect of succumbing to fear in the face of these dangers. Instead, as Catherine believed possible for the western settlers, we can choose a path that leads to life. Like them, we find ourselves in need of faith, of trust in the goodness of the life that has been given to us.

Catherine is a spiritual pioneer who can help us as we develop a new ecology. We are increasingly aware of our need to respond to the suffering of the planet. Many advocate retreat from theologies that support a radical division between matter and spirit. When we imagine the material world to be of spiritual value, we relate to it differently. We allow personal concerns to extend to parts of creation not exclusively concerned with the needs and desires of human beings. We stop treating our home as something that is passing away and, because it has spiritual value, we begin to treat it with more reverence and respect.

As well, we are coming to regard the land less as our property and more as our responsibility. Since the division between the spiritual and material worlds was not part of Catherine's worldview, she did not abandon her responsibility to faithfully care for God's creatures and the local portion of the land, or its people, given into her care. There is much wisdom to be gained by heeding her warnings about social trends that result in overcrowded cities, diminishment of the agricultural way of life, and economies that do not remain locally tied to essential resources and basic industries.

Wandering the forest that Catherine loved to walk in during her days at Camp Morton, it is possible to catch hold of the spirit of a place. In such a natural setting as a woodland path, one must feel one's way along slowly and show respect for the particularities of the environment. Catherine cultivated a practice of spirituality *in* nature and *in* community that beckons us to reverently seek out some similar setting as a place of prayer, meditation, contemplation and action – not as an escape from our worldly concerns, but rather as a place where we might discover something deeper about the true source of our energies and actions, as well as the best places and ways to put them into effect.

These days, when we find ourselves speaking about disorders caused by our separation from the world of nature, when we find ourselves entertaining fears about the dangers our children might encounter in natural environments and in our communities, it is good to pause and consider the validity of Catherine's concern for the small, local community and its environment. This is just as true for city dwellers as it is for people who live in remote and less populated regions. Catherine would have us reflect upon the fact that our relationship with God is also a relationship with our land and its people. Her life inspires us to consider the fruits of daring to live in the spirit of friendship with God, all fellow creatures and the planet we inhabit together.

Notes

1 John Manuel Lozano, "The Charism of the Sisters of Service," revised Sept. 1989, 2.

2 Sr. Kathleen McAlpin, RSM, *Ministry that Transforms: A Contemplative Process of Theological Reflection* (Toronto: Novalis, 2009), 8.

3 Pope John Paul II, "Fides et Ratio," *Encyclical Letter to the Bishops of the Catholic Church* (Rome, 1998), 1.

4 John J. Ó Ríordáin, *The Music of What Happens: Celtic Spirituality – A View from the Inside* (Dublin: Columba Press; Minnesota: St. Mary`s Press, 1996), 56.

5 Ó Ríordáin, *The Music of What Happens*, 35.

6 Richard Schmidt, *God Seekers: Twenty Centuries of Christian Spiritualities* (Grand Rapids, MI: William Eerdmans Publishing, 2008), 60.

7 Patrick Kavanaugh, "The Great Hunger," *Selected Poems* (London: Penguin Books, 1996), 23.

8 Ó Ríordáin, *The Music of What Happens*, 69.

9 Monika K. Hellwig, *Jesus: The Compassion of God* (Wilmington, DE: Michael Glazier, 1983), 42.

10 Jeanne Beck, *To Do and To Endure: The Life of Catherine Donnelly, Sister of Service* (Toronto: Dundurn Press, 1997). 69.

11 Beck, *To Do and To Endure*, 66-67.

12 Richard A. Horsley and Neil Asher Silberman, *The Message and the Kingdom: How Jesus and Paul Ignited a Revolution and Transformed the Ancient World* (Minneapolis: Fortress, 1997), 123–24.

13 Diarmuid O'Murchú, *Our World in Transition: Making Sense of a Changing World* (New York: Crossroad, 1992), 61.

14 Grant Jahnke, OMI, "Sister of Service Paved the Way for Contemporary Religious Life," SOSA, RG1-01, box 8, file 1.

15 Terry A. Veling, *Practical Theology: On Earth as It Is in Heaven* (Maryknoll, NY: Orbis, 2005), 4.

16 Walter Kasper, "Reflection by Cardinal Walter Kasper: Council Clearly Makes Ecumenism Binding as the Work of the Spirit," Vatican website: http://www.vatican.va/roman_curia/pontifical_councils/chrstuni/card-kasper-docs/rc_pc_chrstuni_doc_20031110_unitatis-redintegratio_en.html (Accessed 15 April 2010).

17 Margaret R. Brennan, IHM, *What Was There for Me Once: A Memoir* (Toronto: Novalis, 2009), 50.

18 Brennan, *What Was There for Me Once*, 51.

19 Sister Anne Marie Mongoven, "We Did What the Church Asked Us to Do," 15 August 2009, *National Catholic Reporter*: http://ncronline.org/news/women/we-did-what-church-asked-us-do (Accessed 15 August 2009).

20 Mongoven, "We Did What the Church Asked Us to Do."

21 Jean Vanier, *Becoming Human* (Toronto: Anansi Press, 1998), 95.

22 Gregory Baum, *Political Thought in the Thirties and Forties* (Toronto: James Lorimer and Co., 1980), 31–36.

23 Brennan, *What Was There for Me Once*, 52.

24 Charles E. Curran, *Catholic Social Teaching, 1891 – Present: A Historical, Theological and Ethical Analysis*, Moral Tradition Series, James F. Keenan, Series Editor (Washington, DC: Georgetown University Press, 2002), 5–6.

25 Gregory Baum, *Compassion and Solidarity: The Church for Others* (Toronto: Anansi Press, 1987), 18.

26 Baum, *Compassion and Solidarity*, 19.

27 James D. Whitehead and Evelyn Eaton Whitehead, *Shadows of the Heart: A Spirituality of the Painful Emotions* (New York: Crossroads, 1994), 139.

28 Whitehead and Whitehead, *Shadows of the Heart*, 138–39.

29 Beck, *To Do and To Endure*, 251–52.

30 Philip J. Kennedy, *Catholic Home Missions in Canada: The Beginnings* (Toronto: Catholic Missions in Canada, 2008), 21.

31 Bernhard W. Anderson, *Contours of Old Testament Theology* (Minneapolis: Fortress Press, 1999), 244.

32 Beck, *To Do and To Endure*, 287.

33 Catherine cited the poem in a paper entitled "Application of the Social Teaching of the Church in our Work of Teaching," which was presented to Sisters of Service Teachers in Saskatoon in December of 1960. She did not name the author, but it is likely Douglas Malloch. Credit is given to Malloch for an untitled copy of the poem in the July 31, 1928 *Prescott Evening Courier*.

34 Catherine Donnelly Foundation: http://www.catherinedonnellyfoundation.org/cath.html (Accessed 26 July 2010).

35 Sandra Schneiders, "Call, response and task of prophetic action," part two of a five-part essay: "Religious Life as a Prophetic Life Form" in *National Catholic Reporter*, 4 January 2010: http://ncronline.org/news/women/call-response-and-task-prophetic-action (Accessed 14 February 2010).

36 Wayne A. Meeks, *Christ is the Question* (Louisville, KY: Westminster John Knox Press, 2006), 76–77.

37 Margaret Lavin, *Theology for Ministry* (Ottawa: Novalis, 2004), 140.

38 Charlotte Gray, *Nellie McClung* (Toronto: Penguin Group, 2008), 122.

Bibliography

All of the writings of Catherine Donnelly cited in this work are available through the archives of the Sisters of Service.

Anderson, Bernhard. *Contours of Old Testament Theology*. Minneapolis: Fortress Press, 1999.

Baum, Gregory. *Catholics and Canadian Socialism: Political Thought in the Thirties and Forties*. Toronto: James Lorimer Publishing, 1980.

———. *Compassion and Solidarity: The Church for Others*. Toronto: House of Anansi Press, 1987.

Beck, Jeanne. *To Do and To Endure: The Life of Catherine Donnelly, Sister of Service*. Toronto: Dundurn Press, 1997.

Berry, Wendell. *The Art of the Commonplace: The Agrarian Essays of Wendell Berry*. Edited and introduced by Norman Wirzba. Berkeley, CA: Counterpoint, 2002.

Bloesch, Donald. *Spirituality Old and New: Recovering Authentic Spiritual Life*. Downers Grove, IN: InterVarsity Press, 2007.

Boadt, Lawrence. *Reading the Old Testament: An Introduction*. Mahwah, NJ: Paulist Press, 1984.

Bonhoeffer, Dietrich. *The Cost of Discipleship*. New York: Simon and Schuster, 1959.

Bourke, Mary Carmel, R.S.M. *A Woman Sings of Mercy: Reflections on the Life and Spirit of Mother Catherine McAuley, Foundress of the Sisters of Mercy*. Sydney, Australia: EJ Dwyer, 1987.

Bowe, Barbara. *Biblical Foundations of Spirituality: Touching a Finger to the Flame*. Lanham, MD: Rowman and Littlefield, 2003.

Brennan, Margaret R., IHM. *What Was There for Me Once: A Memoir*. Toronto: Novalis, 2009.

Buechner, Frederick. *Wishful Thinking: A Seeker's ABC*. San Francisco: HarperCollins, 1993.

Crowe, Frederick, SJ. *Appropriating the Lonergan Idea*. Edited by Michael Vertin. Washington, DC: The Catholic University of America Press, 1989.

Curran, Charles. *Catholic Social Teaching, 1891 – Present: A Historical, Theological and Ethical Analysis*. Washington, DC: Georgetown University Press, 2002.

Daly, George. *Catholic Problems in Western Canada*. Toronto: Macmillan, 1921.

De Groot, Christiana and Taylor, Marion Ann, eds. *Recovering Nineteenth Century Women Interpreters of the Bible*. Atlanta: Society of Biblical Literature, 2007.

Fay, Terence A. *A History of Canadian Catholics: Gallicanism, Romanism, and Canadianism*. McGill-Queen's Studies in the History of Religion. Edited by Donald Harman Akenson. Montreal and Kingston: McGill-Queen's University Press, 2002.

Flanner, Austin, OP., ed. *Vatican Council II: Constitutions, Decrees, Declarations: The Basic Sixteen Documents*. New York: Costello, 1996.

Frye, Northrop. *The Great Code: The Bible and Literature*. San Diego: Harcourt, 1982.

Gillese, John Patrick, ed. *Chinook Arch: A Centennial Anthology of Alberta Writing*. Edmonton: The Co-op Press, 1967.

Hathaway, Patricia Cooney. *Weaving Faith and Experience: A Woman's Perspective*. Cincinnati: St. Anthony Messenger Press, 2010.

Hellwig, Monika. *Jesus: The Compassion of God: New Perspectives on the Tradition of Christianity*. Wilmington, Delaware: Michael Glazier, 1983.

Horsley, Richard A. and Silberman, Neil Asher. *The Message and the Kingdom: How Jesus and Paul Ignited a Revolution and Transformed the Ancient World*. Minneapolis: Fortress Press, 1997.

John Paul II. *Fides et Ratio*. Encyclical Letter to the Bishops of the Roman Catholic Church. Rome, 1998.

Julian of Norwich. *Revelations of Divine Love*. Translated by Elizabeth Spearing. New York: Penguin Books, 1998.

Kasper, Walter. "Reflection by Cardinal Walter Kasper: Council Clearly Makes Ecumenism Binding as the Work of the Spirit," Vatican website: http://www.vatican.va/roman_curia/pontifical_councils/chrstuni/card-kasper-docs/rc_pc_chrstuni_doc_20031110_unitatis-redintegratio_en.html (Accessed 15 April 2010).

Kavanaugh, Patrick. *Selected Poems*. Edited and with an introduction by Antionette Quinn. London: Penguin Books, 1996.

Kennedy, Philip J. *Catholic Home Missions in Canada: The Beginnings*. Toronto, Ontario: Catholic Missions in Canada, 2008.

La Cugna, Catherine Mowry, ed. *Freeing Theology: The Essentials of Theology in Feminist Perspective*. New York: HarperCollins, 1993.

Laverdure, Paul. *Redemption and Renewal: The Redemptorists of English Canada, 1834–1994*. Toronto and Oxford: Dundurn Press, 1996.

Lavin, Margaret. *Theology for Ministry*. Ottawa: Novalis, 2004.

Magray, Mary Peckham. *The Transforming Power of Nuns: Women, Religion, and Cultural Change in Ireland*. New York and Oxford: Oxford University Press, 1998.

McAlpin, Kathleen, RSM. *Ministry that Transforms: A Contemplative Process of Theological Reflection*. Toronto: Novalis, 2009.

McFague, Sallie. *The Body of God: An Ecological Theology.* Minneapolis: Fortress Press, 1993.

―――. *Models of God: Theology for an Ecological, Nuclear Age.* Philadelphia: Fortress Press, 1987.

Meeks, Wayne. *Christ is the Question.* Louisville, KY: Westminster John Knox Press, 2006.

Metz, Johannes Baptist. *Poverty of Spirit.* New York: Paulist Press, 1968.

Mongoven, Anne Marie. "We Did What the Church Asked Us to Do," 15 August 2009, *National Catholic Reporter*, http://ncronline. org/news/women-religious/we-did-what-church-asked-us-do (Accessed 14 December 2012).

Ó Murchú, Diarmuid. *Our World in Transition: Making Sense of a Changing World.* New York: Crossroads, 1992.

Ó Ríordáin, John, C.Ss.R. *The Music of What Happens: Celtic Spirituality – A View from the Inside.* Dublin: Columba Press; Minnesota: St. Mary's Press, 1996.

Rolheiser, Ronald, OMI. *The Holy Longing: The Search for Christian Spirituality.* New York: Doubleday, 1999.

Rush, Ormond. *Still Interpreting Vatican II: Some Hermeneutical Principles.* Mahwah, NJ: Paulist Press, 2004.

Schmidt, Richard H. *God Seekers: Twenty Centuries of Christian Spiritualities.* Grand Rapids, MI: William Eerdmans Publishing, 2008.

Schneiders, Sandra. "Call, response and task of prophetic action," part two of a five-part essay: "Religious Life as a Prophetic Life Form" in *National Catholic Reporter*, 4 January 2010: http://ncronline. org/news/women-religious/religious-life-prophetic-life-form (Accessed 14 December 2012).

Sheridan, E.F. SJ, ed. *Do Justice! The Social Teaching of the Canadian Catholic Bishops, 1945-1986.* Toronto: Jesuit Centre for Social Faith and Justice, 1987.

Soëlle, Dorothy. *The Silent Cry: Mysticism and Resistance.* Translated by Barbara and Martin Rumsscheidt. Minneapolis: Fortress Press, 2001.

Tillich, Paul. *Dynamics of Faith.* New York: Harper and Row, 1957.

Tobin, Thomas H., SJ. *The Spirituality of Paul.* Wilmington, DE: Michael Glazier, 1987.

Vanier, Jean. *Becoming Human.* Toronto: House of Anansi Press, 1998.

Veling, Terry A. *A Practical Theology: On Earth as It Is in Heaven.* Maryknoll, NY: Orbis Books, 2005.

Whitehead, James and Evelyn. *Shadows of the Heart: A Spirituality of the Painful Emotions.* New York: Crossroads, 1994.

Wink, Walter. *The Powers that Be: Theology for a New Millennium.* New York: Galilee, 1998.